LATIN'S NOT SO TOUGH!

**LEVEL ONE
ANSWER KEY**

A Classical Latin Worktext
by
Karen Mohs

Dear Parent/Teacher:

This answer key is designed to assist you in teaching Latin Workbook Level One.

Daily flashcard practice is essential. Please do not neglect this effective learning tool. The letters for flashcard use are located at the end of the workbook.

Most importantly, make this an enjoyable learning experience and a happy memory for both you and your student.

References for this series include *First Year Latin* by Charles Jenney, Jr., *Second Year Latin* by Charles Jenney, Jr., and *The New College Latin & English Dictionary* by John C. Traupman, Ph.D.

ISBN 1-931842-51-5

Greek 'n' Stuff
P.O. Box 882
Moline, IL 61266-0882
www.greeknstuff.com

Revised 9/04

SCHEDULE OF LESSONS
(PROPOSAL FOR LEVEL ONE)

In overview, the *Latin's Not So Tough!* workbooks are designed such that the student ideally completes one page per day (and practices his or her flashcards each day as well). (It should be noted that older students often complete more than one page per day when they are working in the early levels.) The workbooks were not designed within a framework of "lessons." Many parents have told us they appreciate this approach. It is easy to follow, without need of additional parent/teacher preparation and scheduling.

However, some parents/teachers prefer the "lesson" approach. Please be aware that this "Schedule of Lessons" is an artificial grid placed over a series not written with this grid in mind. The assigned pages are arbitrary and should be modified so the student can progress through the workbooks at a pace suitable to his or her age/skill level.

A note about our methodology:
      Referred to by some as the "Saxon of Latin," this series begins gently and advances gradually, providing plenty of reinforcement through a wide variety of workbook activities and translation exercises. By introducing new concepts slowly, *Latin's Not So Tough!* avoids the pitfall common to many foreign language courses whereby the student suddenly faces a steep learning curve, becomes frustrated, fails to internalize the language, and develops an aversion to foreign language study in general. The overwhelming response from those using *Latin's Not So Tough!* can be summed up by the words we hear so often: "This is my student's favorite subject."

Lesson 1
      Pages 1-4 - Alphabet letters A̅a̅ and Aɑ

> *Teacher tip:*
>   *Latin's Not So Tough!* teaches classical pronunciation. Because the distinctions between classical and ecclesiastical pronunciations are relatively minor, students generally do not find it difficult to switch from one pronunciation to another. For a comparison of the classical and ecclesiastical pronunciations, see pages 4-6 of *The New College Latin & English Dictionary* by John C. Traupman, Ph.D. For a thorough examination of pronunciation, see pages 1-8 of *New Latin Grammar* by Charles E. Bennett or pages 1-6 of *Latin Grammar* by B.L. Gildersleeve & G. Lodge.

Lesson 2
      Pages 5-8 - Alphabet letters Bb and Cc

Lesson 3
Pages 9-12 - Alphabet letters Dd and Ēē

Lesson 4
Pages 13-16 - Alphabet letters Ee and Ff

Lesson 5
Pages 17-20 - Alphabet letters Gg and Hh

Lesson 6
Pages 21-24 - Alphabet letters Ĭĭ and Ii

Lesson 7
Pages 25-28 - Alphabet letters Kk and Ll

Lesson 8
Pages 29-32 - Alphabet letters Mm and Nn

****
QUIZ #1 (optional)
****

Lesson 9
Pages 33-36 - Alphabet letters Ōō and Oo

Lesson 10
Pages 37-40 - Alphabet letters Pp and Qq

Lesson 11
Pages 41-44 - Alphabet letters Rr and Ss

Lesson 12
Pages 45-48 - Alphabet letters Tt and Ūū

Lesson 13
Pages 49-52 - Alphabet letters Uu and Vv

Lesson 14
Pages 53-56 - Alphabet letters Xx and Ȳȳ

Lesson 15
Pages 57-60 - Alphabet letters Yy and Zz

Lesson 16
Pages 61-62 - Alphabet practice

****
QUIZ #4 (optional)
****

****
FINAL EXAM (optional)
****

Appendix

Latin Workbook - Level 1
Copyright © 1996 by Karen Mohs

Ā* ā

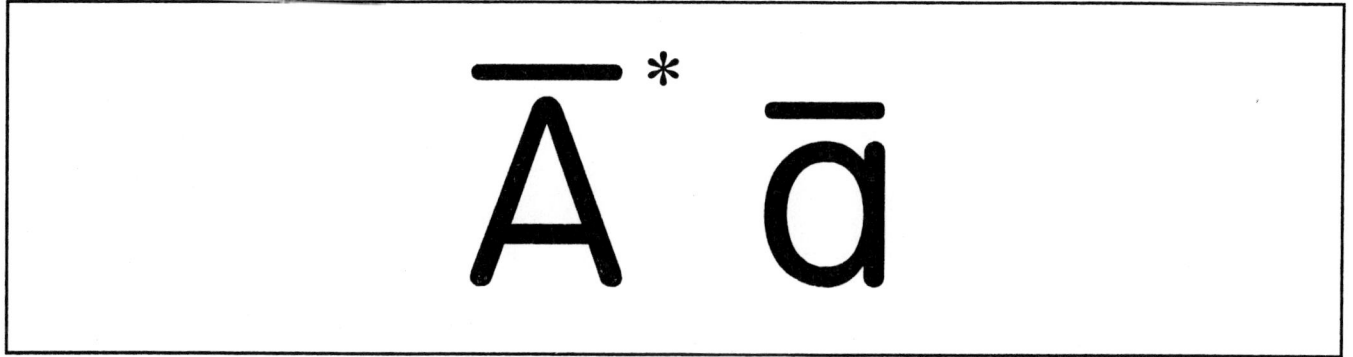

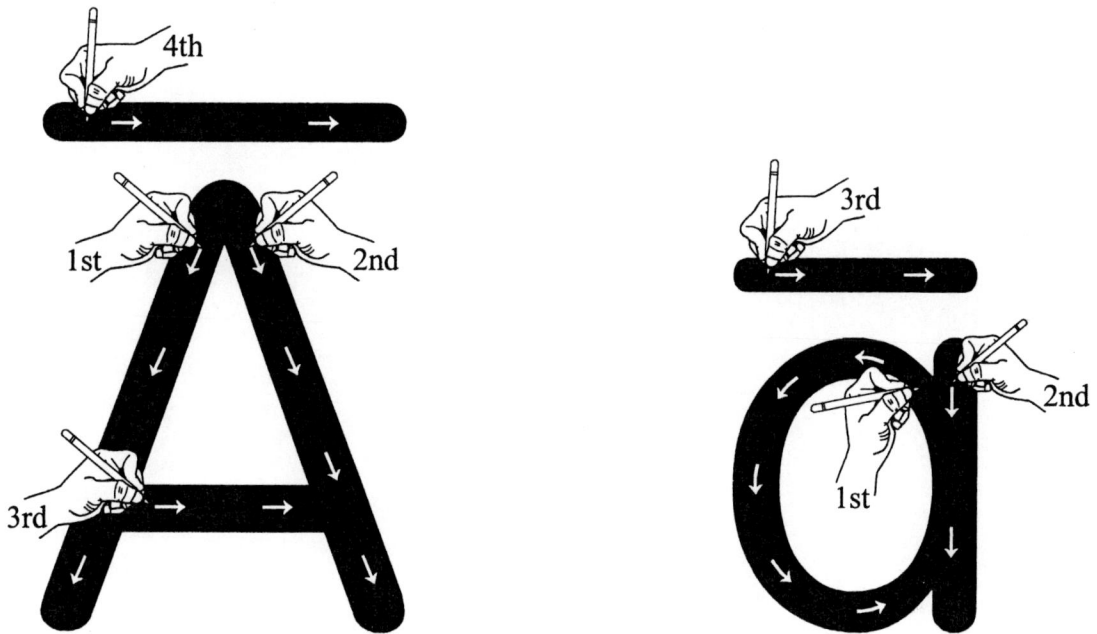

Write the letters across each line.
As you write them, say the sound of "**a**" in *father*.

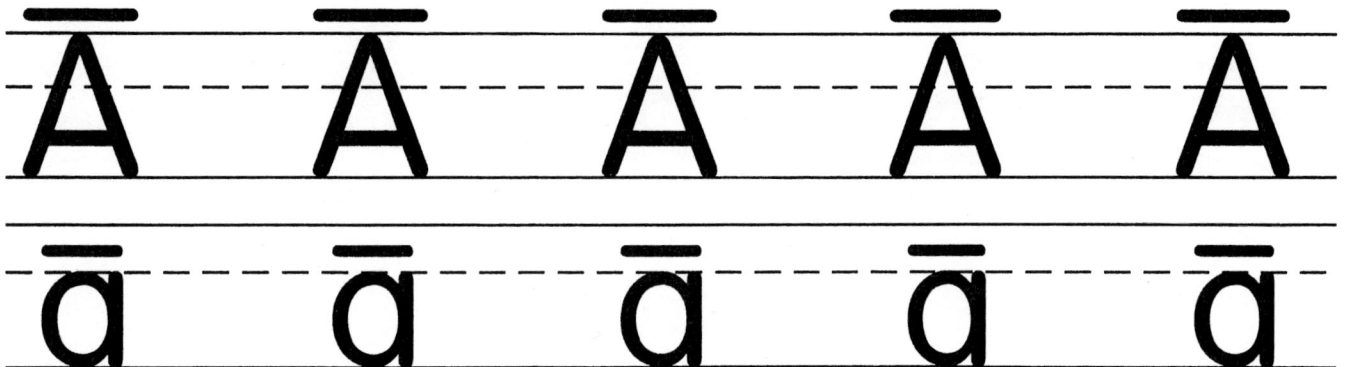

Ā Ā Ā Ā Ā

ā ā ā ā ā

*The short line above certain Latin vowels is called a *macron*.

Circle the words that have the ā sound.

(mark)   quaint

(calm)   jacket

nail   (darn)

(garden)   battle

ham   (hurrah)

pale   (salsa)

A a

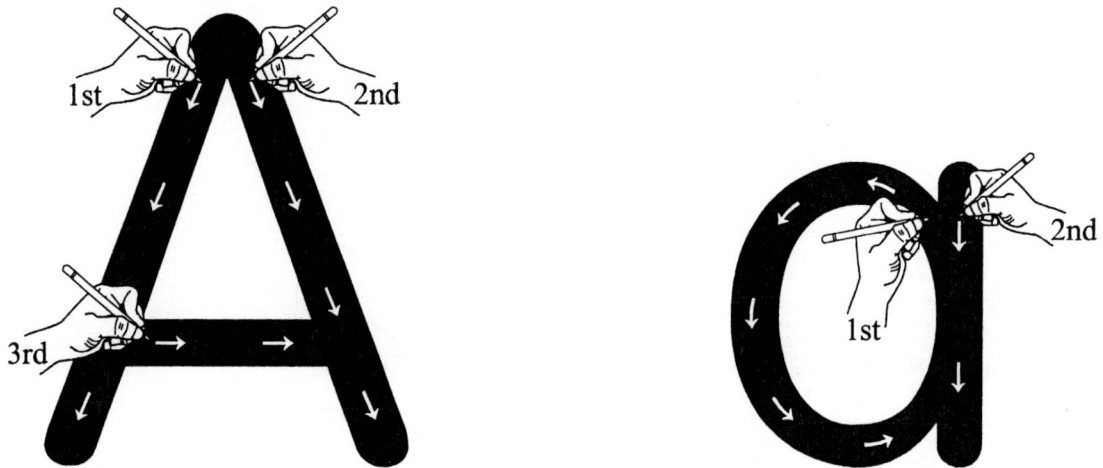

Write the letters across each line.
As you write them, say the sound of "**a**" in *idea*.

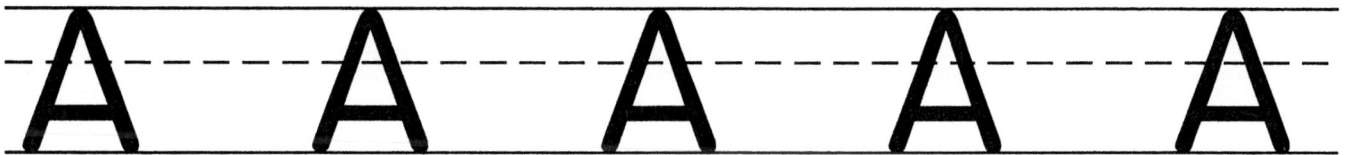

A A A A A A

a a a a a a

You now know two letters of the Latin alphabet. Start your flashcard deck with these letters and practice them every day.
(See back of workbook for flashcards.)

☐ I practiced my flashcards today.

Draw a line from the letter to its sound.

ɑ   **a** in *father*

ā   **a** in *idea*

Circle the words that have the ɑ sound.

(canoe)   far

arch   (alike)

math   (ravine)

(soda)   ace

☐ I practiced my flashcards today.

Latin Workbook - Level 1
Copyright © 1996 by Karen Mohs

B b

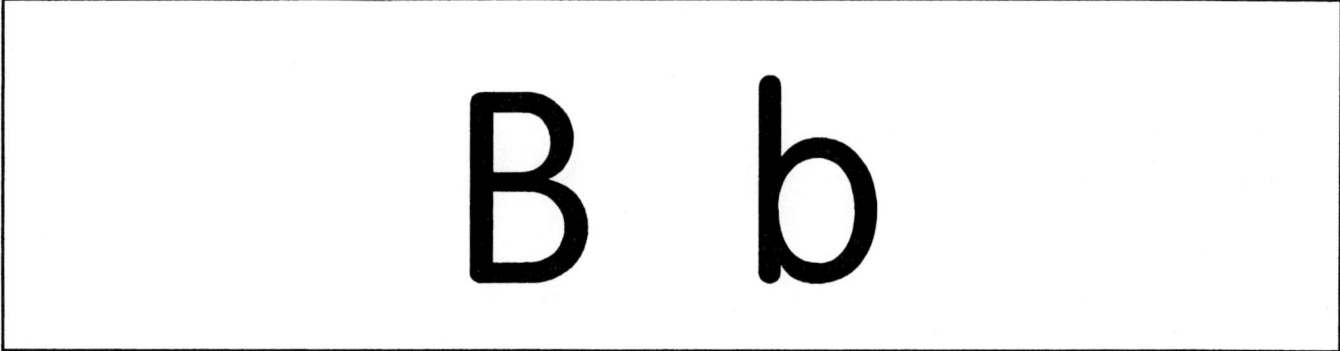

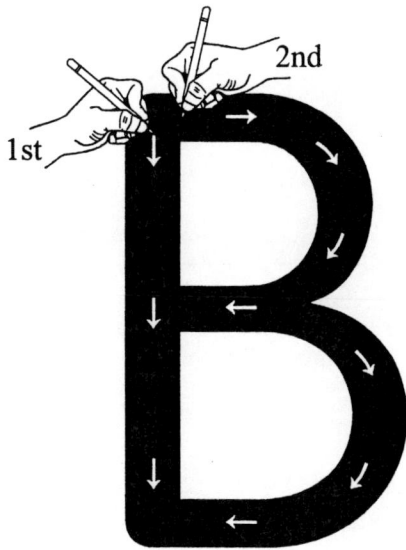

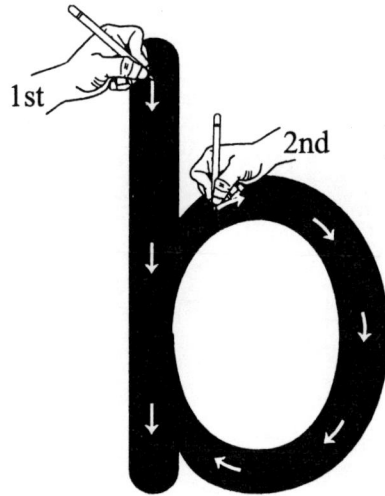

Write the letters across each line.
As you write them, say the sound of "**b**" in *boy*.

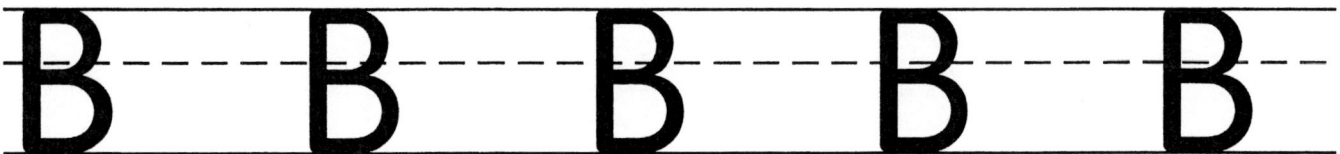

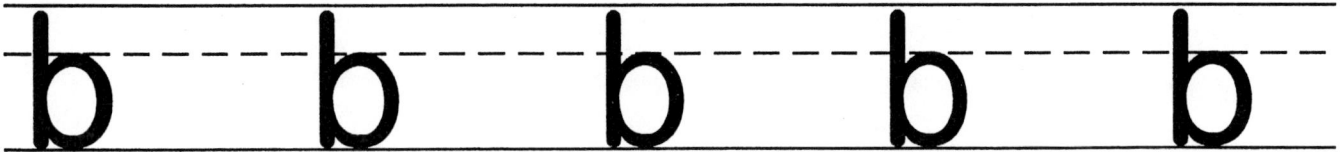

B   B   B   B   B

b   b   b   b   b

☐   I practiced my flashcards today.
(Remember to add this new card to your flashcards.)

REMEMBER!
B or b sounds like **b** in *boy*.

Circle the words that have the sound at the beginning of the row.

ā	cat (jar)	(star) rash	haste (father)
a	gag (along)	bat (afar)	wait (salad)
b	(box) cook	(bed) sprain	kick (bat)
ā	safe (far)	tank (sparkle)	(scarf) pack
a	(arise) plate	(along) drag	jam (away)

☐ I practiced my flashcards today.

Latin Workbook - Level 1
Copyright © 1996 by Karen Mohs

C c

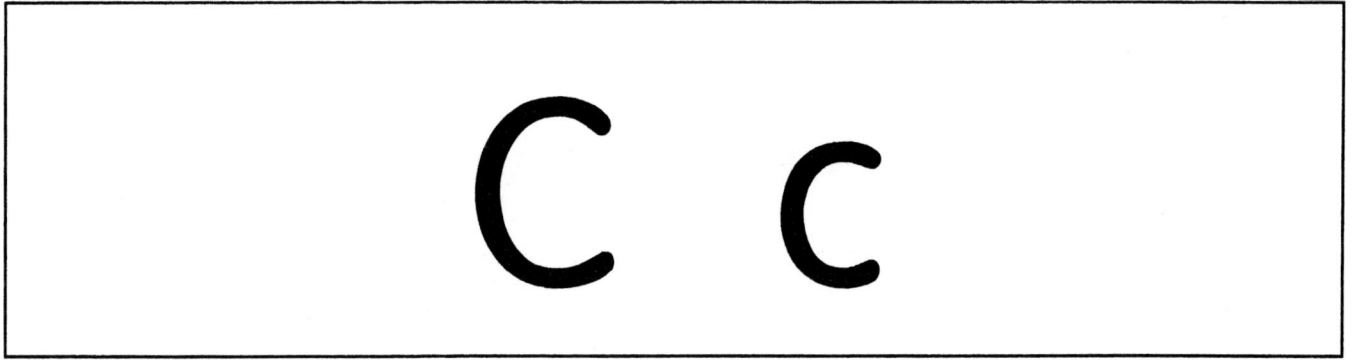

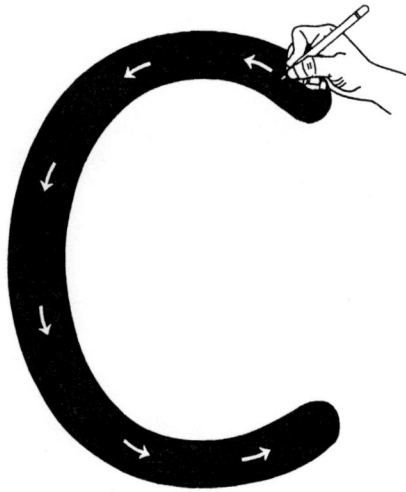

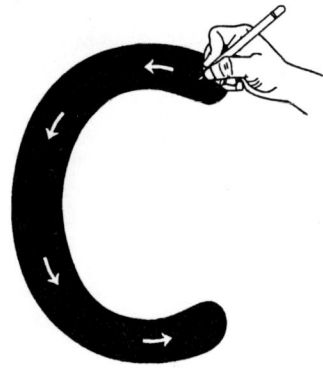

Write the letters across each line.
As you write them, say the sound of "**c**" in *cat*.

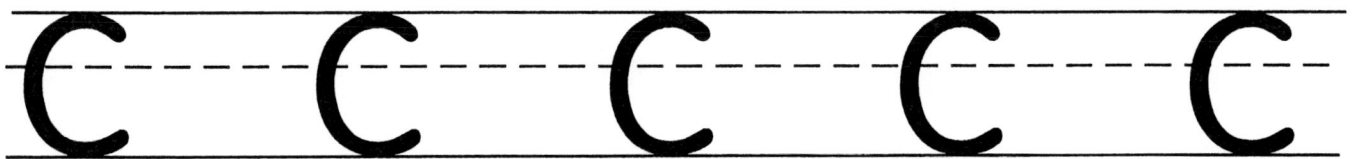

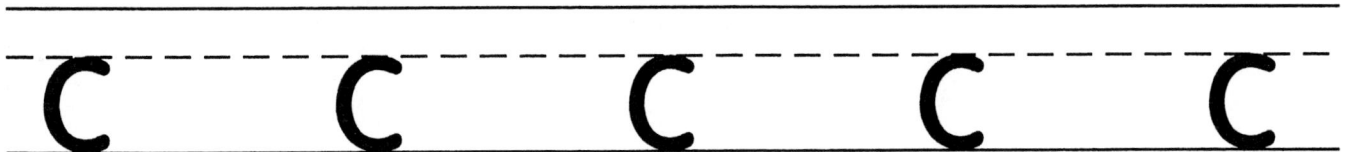

C C C C C

C C C C C

☐ I practiced my flashcards today.
(Remember to add this new card to your flashcards.)

Draw a line from the Latin letter to its sound.

ā   **b** in *boy*

b   **c** in *cat*

a   **a** in *father*

c   **a** in *idea*

Circle the words that have the Latin c sound.

city

cane

cedar

cat

cell

come

cup

cost

center

cinder

cub

coat

cent

I practiced my flashcards today.

Latin Workbook - Level 1
Copyright © 1996 by Karen Mohs

D d

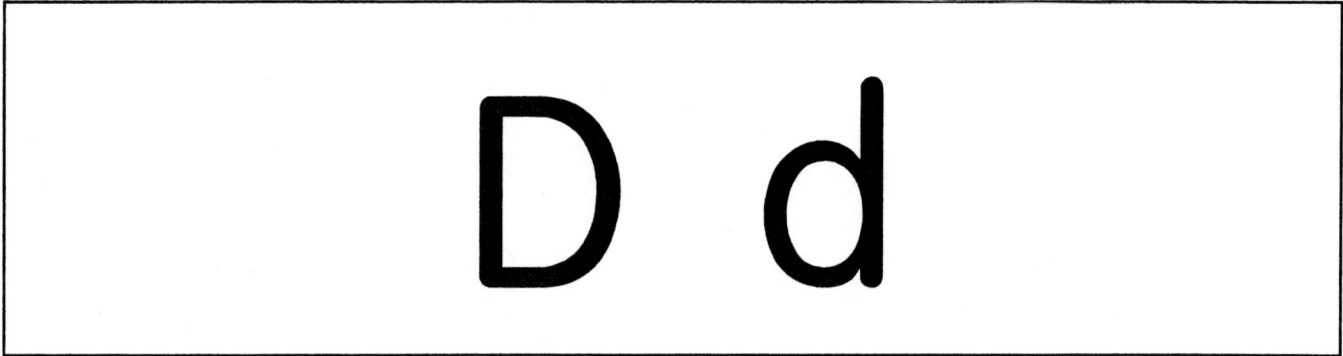

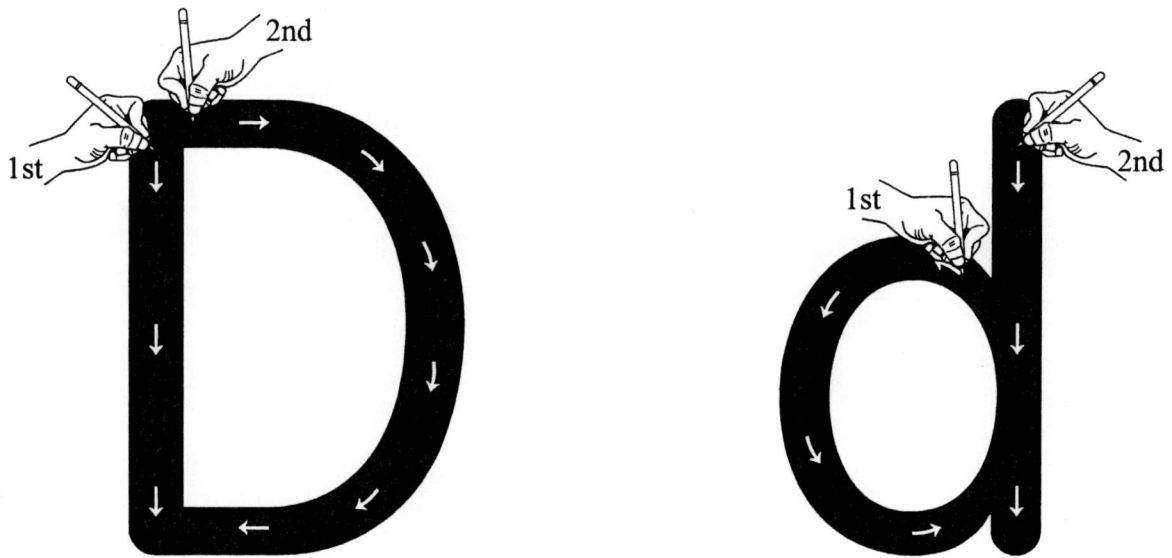

Write the letters across each line.
As you write them, say the sound of "**d**" in *dog*.

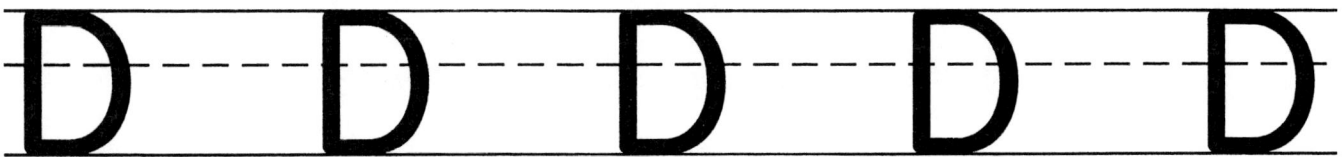

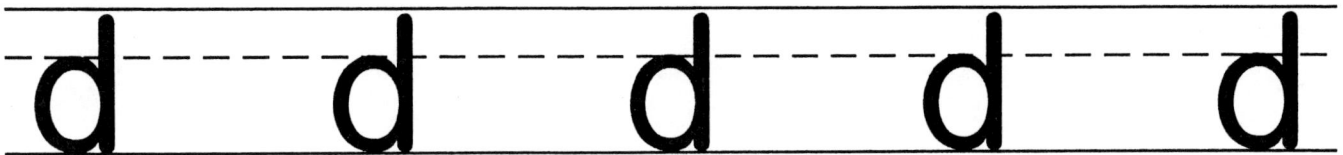

D   D   D   D   D

d   d   d   d   d

☐ I practiced my flashcards today.
(Remember to add this new card to your flashcards.)

REMEMBER!
D or d sounds like **d** in *dog*.

Circle *yes* if the sentence is true. Circle *no* if it is not true.

(yes) *no* 1. The Latin letter b sounds like the **b** in *boy*.

yes (no) 2. The Latin letter ā sounds like the **a** in *cape*.

yes (no) 3. The Latin letter c sounds like the **c** in *cent*.

(yes) *no* 4. The Latin letter ā sounds like the **a** in *father*.

yes (no) 5. The Latin letter a sounds like the **a** in *sat*.

(yes) *no* 6. The Latin letter d sounds like the **d** in *dog*.

☐ I practiced my flashcards today.

Latin Workbook - Level 1
Copyright © 1996 by Karen Mohs

Ē ē

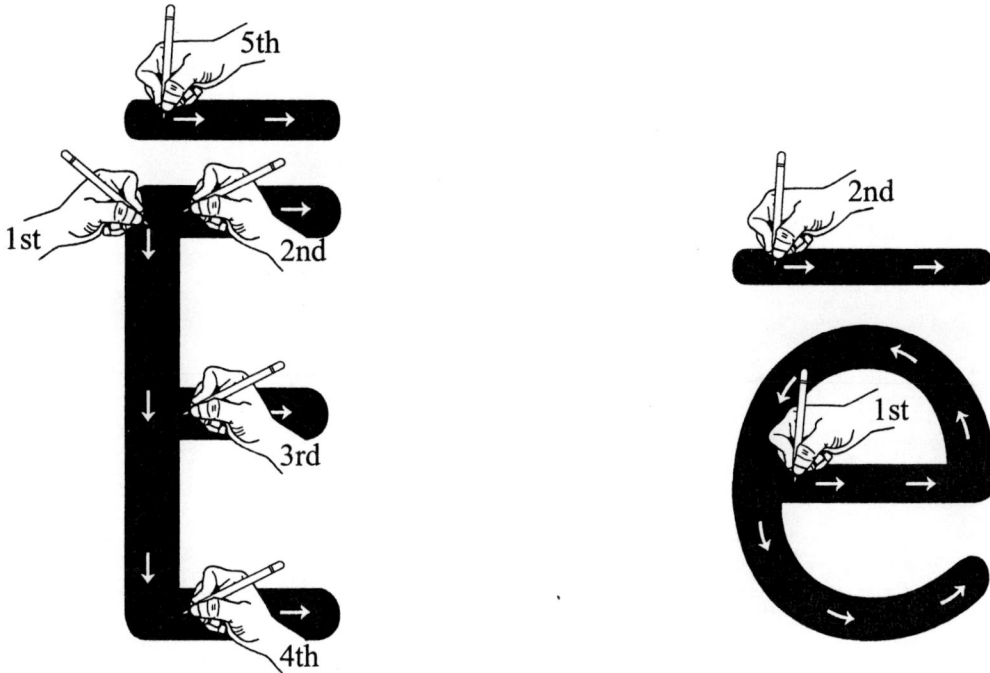

Write the letters across each line.
As you write them, say the sound of "**ey**" in *obey*.

Ē   Ē   Ē   Ē   Ē

ē   ē   ē   ē   ē

☐ I practiced my flashcards today.
(Remember to add this new card to your flashcards.)

REMEMBER!
Ē or ē sounds like **ey** in *obey*.

Fill in the blanks with the missing lowercase Latin letters.

1. Latin ___b___ sounds like the **b** in *boy*.

2. Latin ___ē___ sounds like the **ey** in *obey*.

3. Latin ___c___ sounds like the **c** in *cat*.

4. Latin ___ā___ sounds like the **a** in *father*.

5. Latin ___a___ sounds like the **a** in *idea*.

6. Latin ___d___ sounds like the **d** in *dog*.

☐ I practiced my flashcards today.

E e

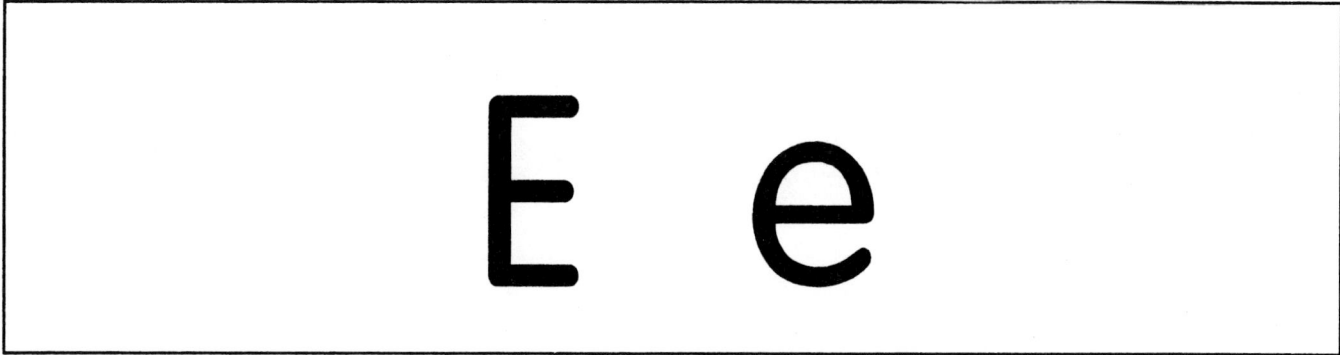

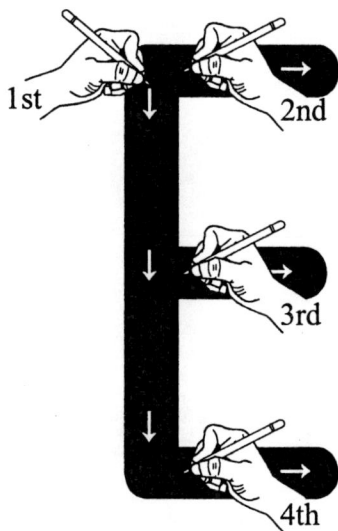

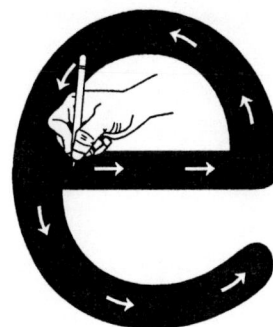

Write the letters across each line.
As you write them, say the sound of "**e**" in ***bet***.

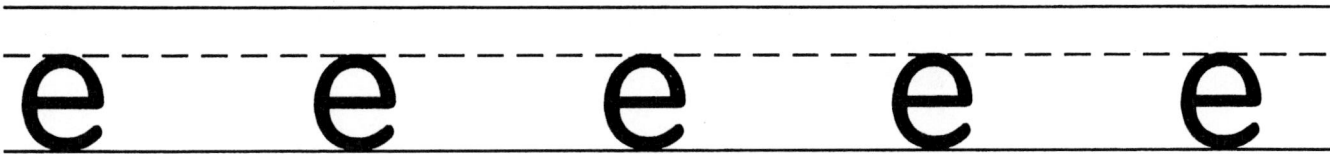

E E E E E E

e e e e e

☐ I practiced my flashcards today.
(Remember to add this new card to your flashcards.)

REMEMBER!
E or e sounds like **e** in *bet*.

Write the words under the correct Latin sounds.

get	wet	stay	bless
brake	step	weigh	grace

ē

stay
brake
weigh
grace

e

get
wet
bless
step

☐ I practiced my flashcards today.

Latin Workbook - Level 1
Copyright © 1996 by Karen Mohs

F f

1st 2nd 3rd

1st 2nd

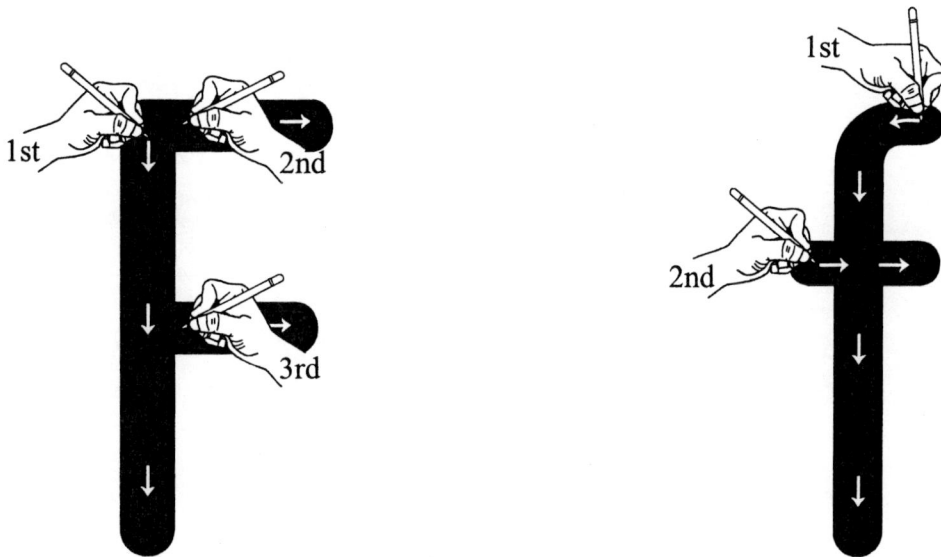

Write the letters across each line.
As you write them, say the sound of **"f"** in *fan*.

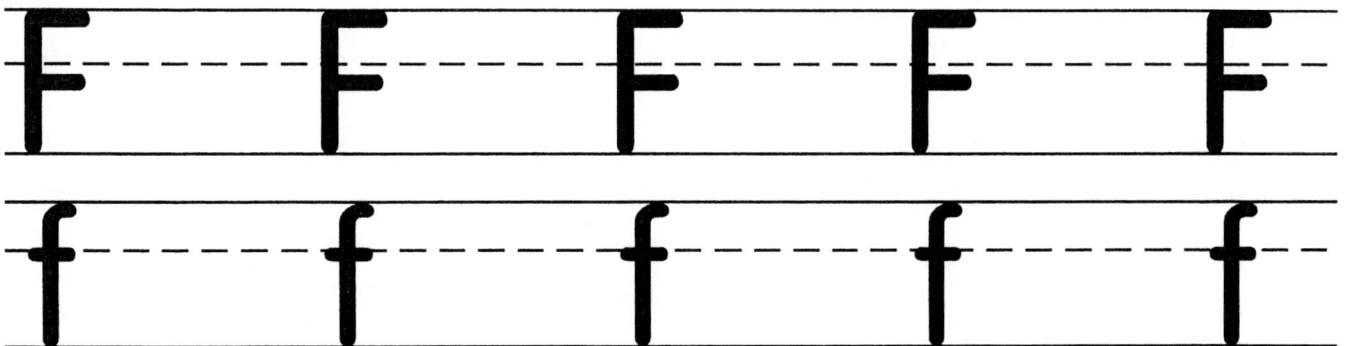

F F F F F

f f f f f

☐ I practiced my flashcards today.
(Remember to add this new card to your flashcards.)

> # REMEMBER!
> ## F or f sounds like **f** in *fan*.

Match the Latin letters with their sounds.

c   a in *father*

f   e in *get*

e   c in *cat*

ā   f in *fan*

b ——————— b in *boy*

ē   d in *dog*

a   ey in *obey*

d   a in *idea*

☐ I practiced my flashcards today.

G g

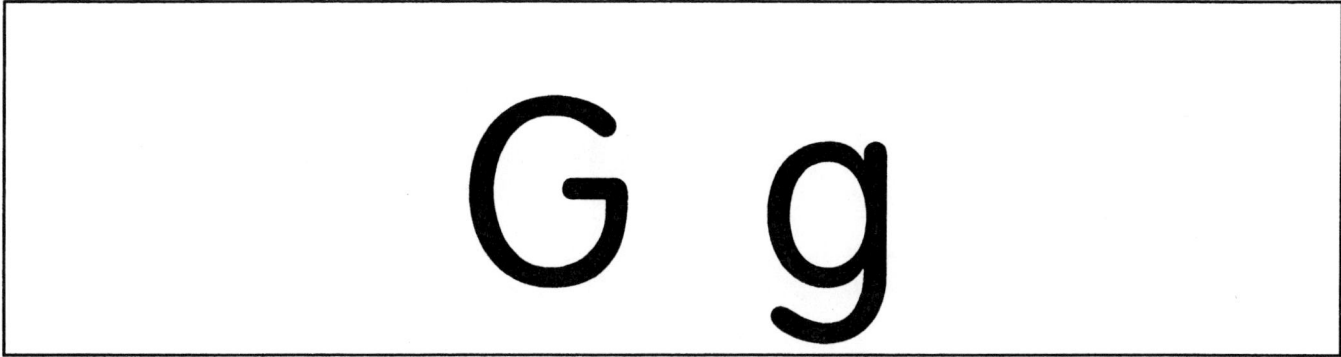

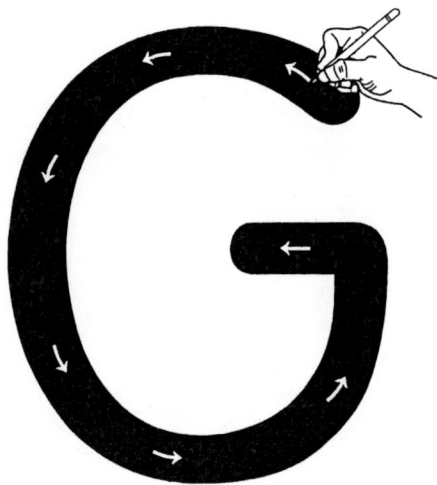

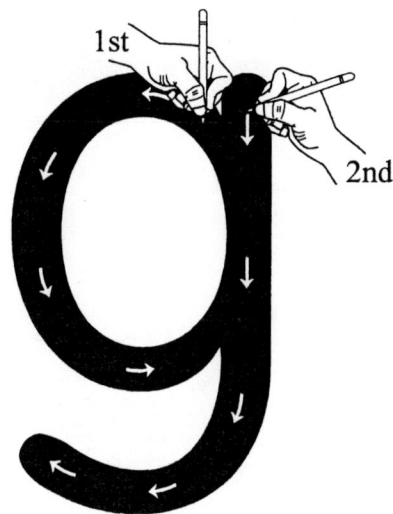

Write the letters across each line.
As you write them, say the sound of "**g**" in *go*.

G G G G G

g g g g g

☐ I practiced my flashcards today.
(Remember to add this new card to your flashcards.)

REMEMBER!
G or g sounds like **g** in ***go***.

Look at the Latin letter in the corner of the box.
Circle the words that have the sound it makes.

e
- (wet)
- deep
- (head)
- (thread)
- reap

c
- (cash)
- percent
- cease
- (catch)
- (cable)

f
- very
- (fact)
- even
- (fish)
- (fever)

ē
- (may)
- key
- (wave)
- eye
- (braid)

g
- ginger
- (fig)
- (geese)
- age
- (gray)

d
- (dust)
- (red)
- (day)
- baby
- map

☐ I practiced my flashcards today.

Latin Workbook - Level 1
Copyright © 1996 by Karen Mohs

H h

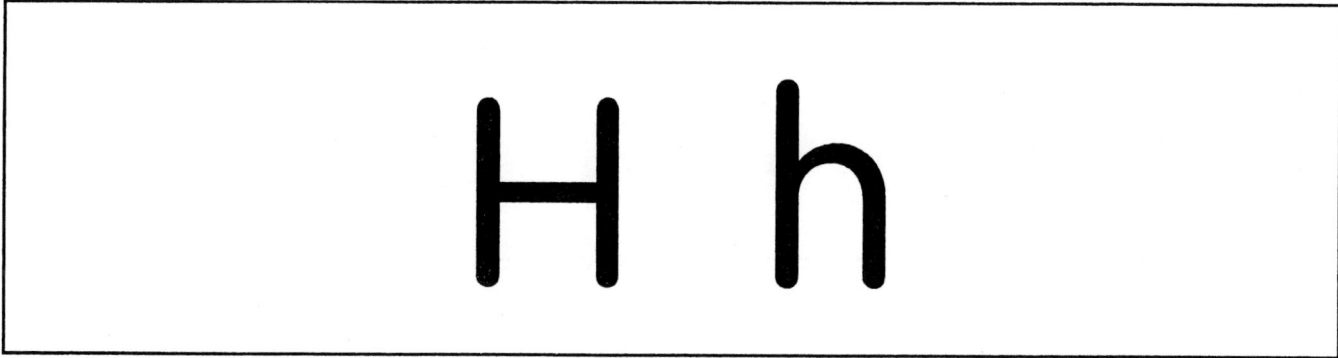

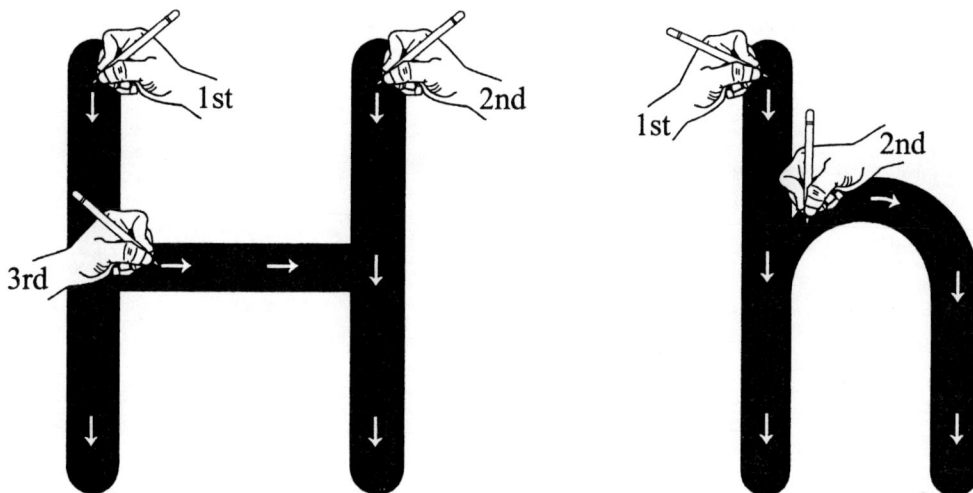

Write the letters across each line.
As you write them, say the sound of "**h**" in *hat*.

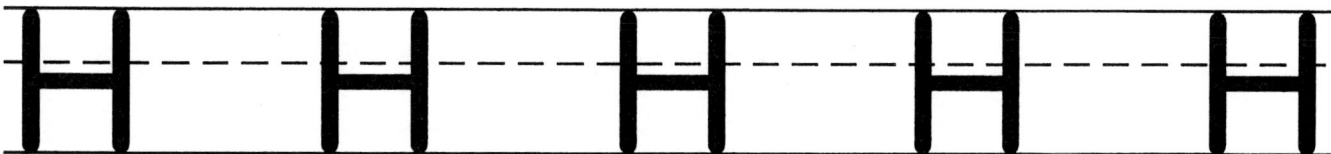

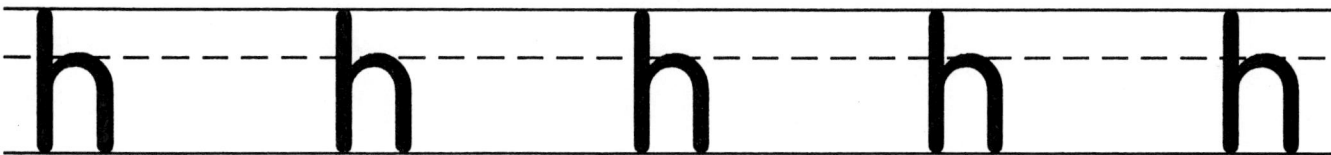

H H H H H

h h h h h

☐ I practiced my flashcards today.
(Remember to add this new card to your flashcards.)

REMEMBER!
H or h sounds like **h** in *hat*.

Circle the letters that match the sound in the big box.

g in *go*	b	b	(g)	c
	(g)	c	b	(g)
h in *hat*	(h)	g	(h)	b
	a	d	b	(h)
ey in *obey*	e	ā	e	(ē)
	a	(ē)	ā	e
e in *get*	i	ē	(e)	ē
	(e)	a	(e)	a
f in *fan*	(f)	t	(f)	l
	l	(f)	l	t

☐ I practiced my flashcards today.

Latin Workbook - Level 1
Copyright © 1996 by Karen Mohs

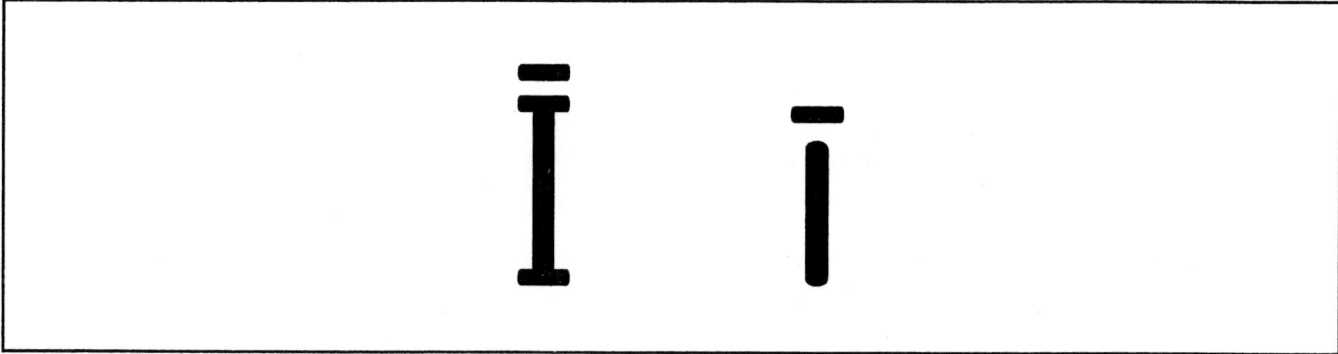

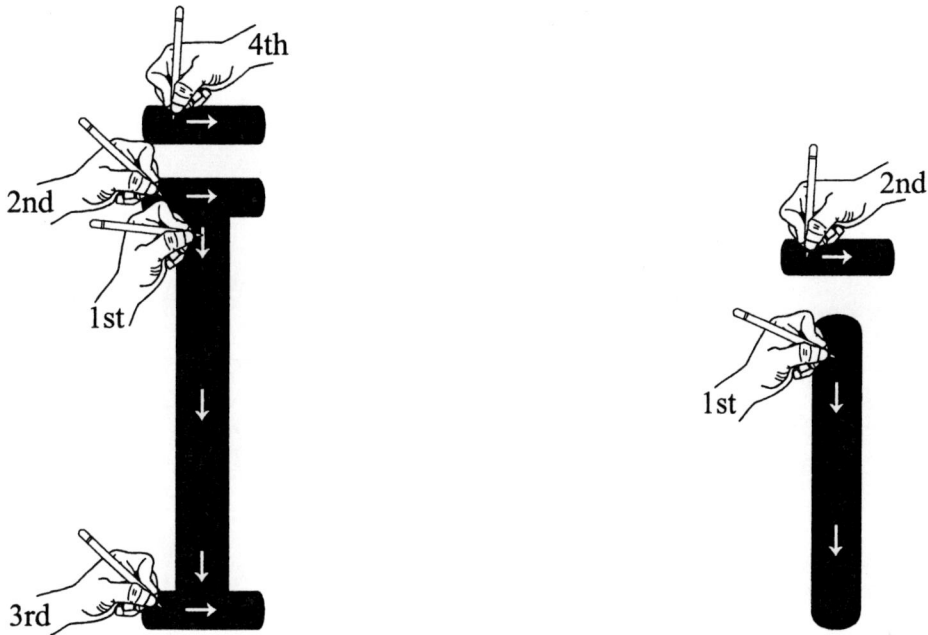

Write the letters across each line.
As you write them, say the sound of "i" in *machine*.

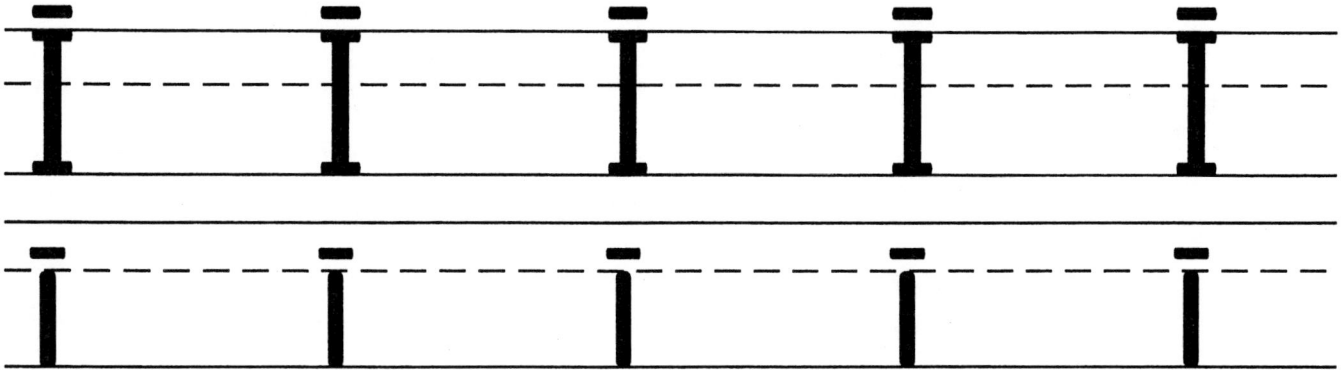

☐ I practiced my flashcards today.
(Remember to add this new card to your flashcards.)

REMEMBER!
Ī or ī sounds like **i** in *machine*.

Fill in the blanks with the missing lowercase Latin letters.

1. Latin __h__ sounds like the **h** in *hat*.

2. Latin __f__ sounds like the **f** in *fan*.

3. Latin __ē__ sounds like the **ey** in *obey*.

4. Latin __g__ sounds like the **g** in *go*.

5. Latin __ī__ sounds like the **i** in *machine*.

6. Latin __e__ sounds like the **e** in *get*.

☐ I practiced my flashcards today.

Latin Workbook - Level 1
Copyright © 1996 by Karen Mohs

I i

2nd
1st
3rd

2nd
1st

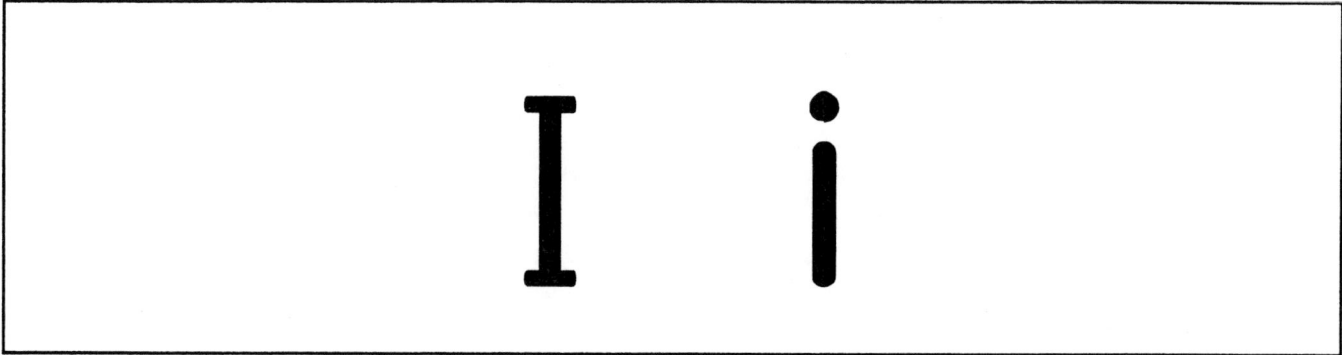

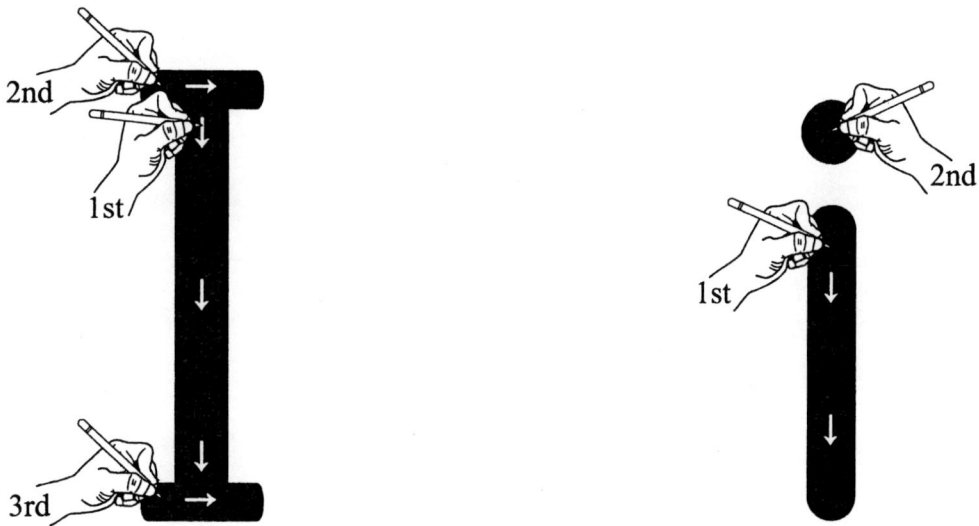

Write the letters across each line.
As you write them, say the sound of "i" in *sit*.

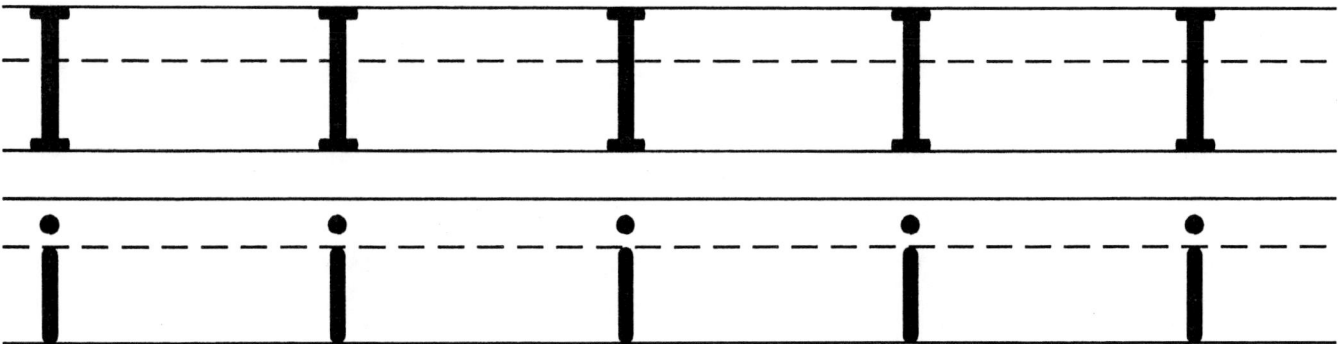

I   I   I   I   I

i   i   i   i   i

☐ I practiced my flashcards today.
(Remember to add this new card to your flashcards.)

REMEMBER!
I or i sounds like **i** in *sit*.

Write the words under the correct Latin sounds.

green	street	miss	mean
sip	bit	free	grin

ī	i
green	miss
street	sip
mean	bit
free	grin

☐ I practiced my flashcards today.

Latin Workbook - Level 1
Copyright © 1996 by Karen Mohs

K k

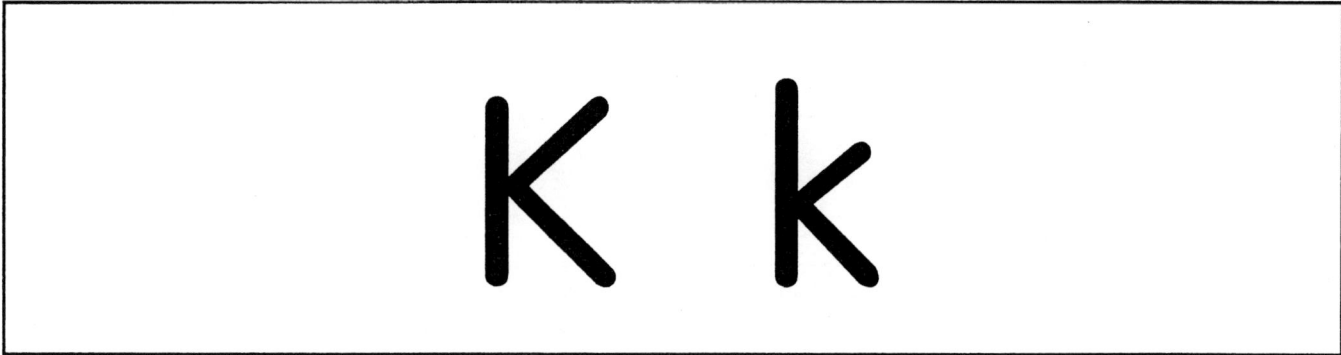

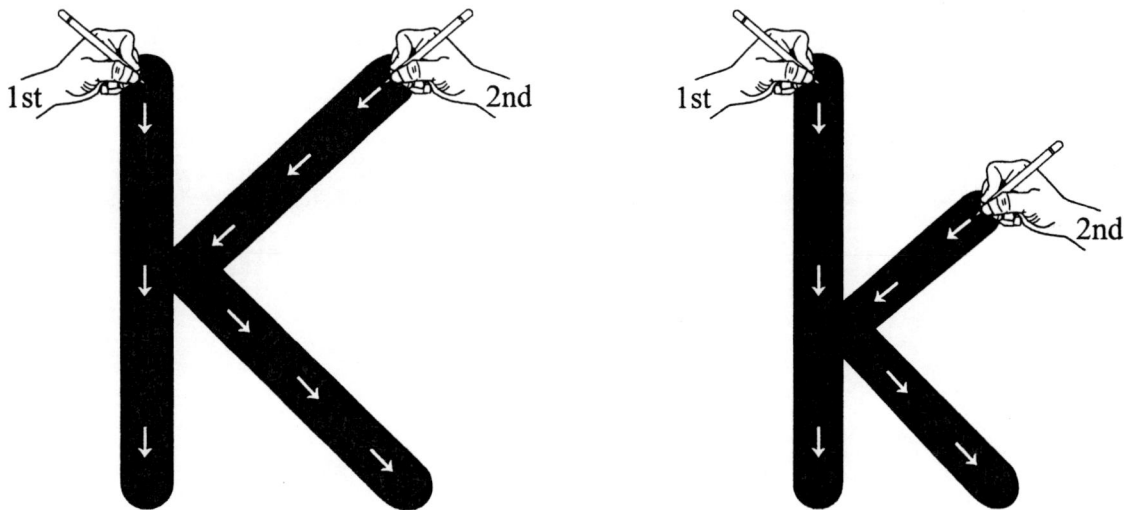

Write the letters across each line.
As you write them, say the sound of "**k**" in *king*.

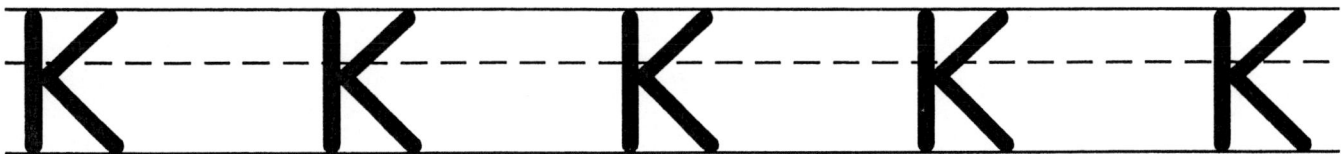

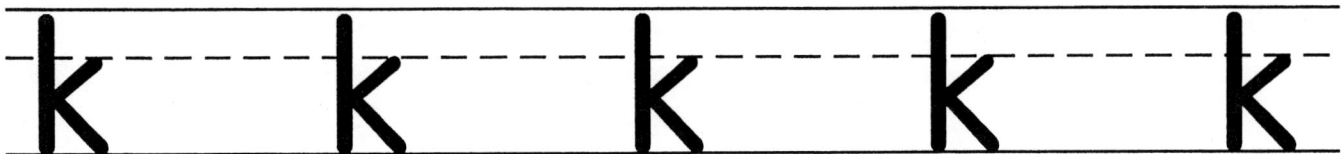

K   K   K   K   K

k   k   k   k   k

☐ I practiced my flashcards today.
(Remember to add this new card to your flashcards.)

Circle the words that have the sound of the Latin letter at the beginning of the row.

i	(sit)	shut	(dish)
k	slice	(kiss)	(king)
b	hood	(boy)	(baby)
c	(cook)	(cat)	rice
ā	crane	(barn)	(father)
g	(go)	(give)	gem
ē	seat	(ray)	(obey)
ī	(bean)	light	(machine)
f	cave	(fan)	(food)
h	(him)	(hat)	this
e	(get)	ate	(west)

☐ I practiced my flashcards today.

L l

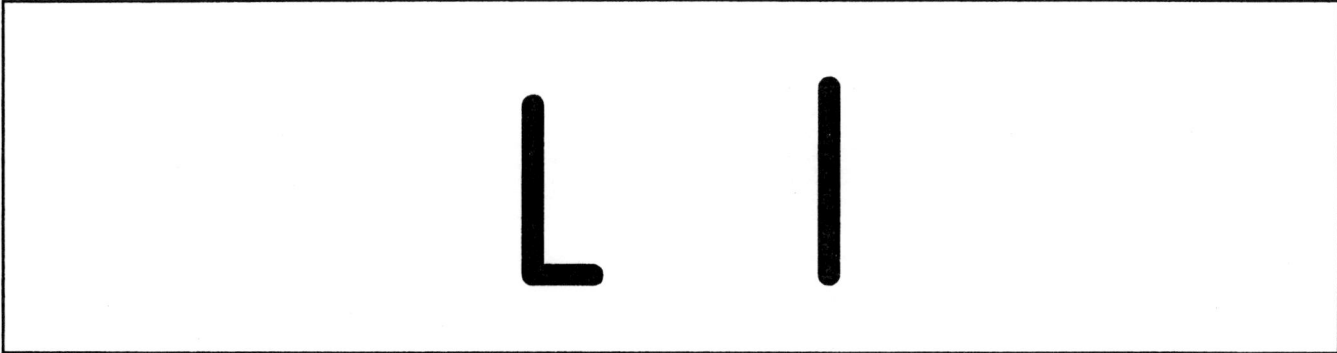

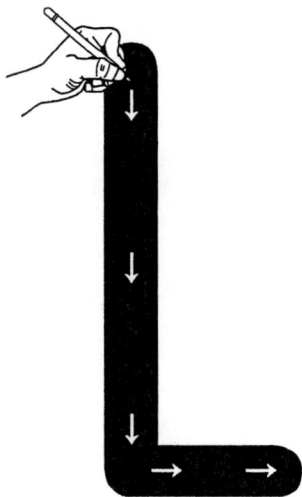

Write the letters across each line.
As you write them, say the sound of "l" in *land*.

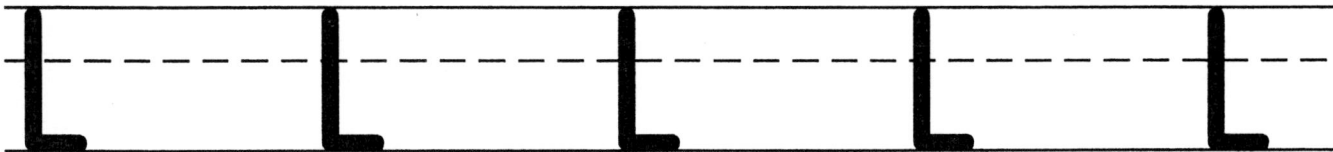

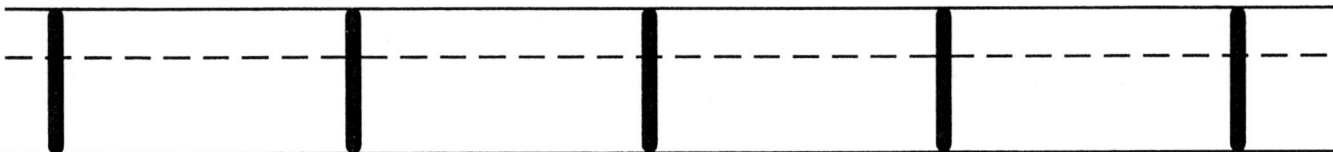

☐ I practiced my flashcards today.
(Remember to add this new card to your flashcards.)

REMEMBER!
L or l sounds like l in *land*.

Color the triangle if the Latin letter matches the sound.

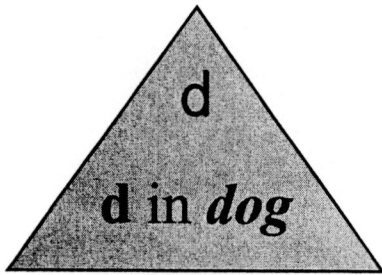

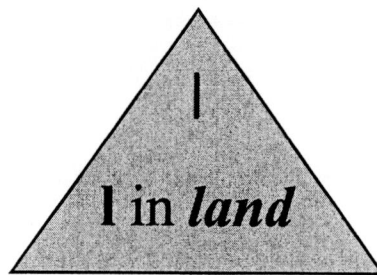

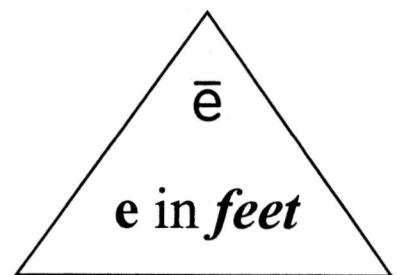

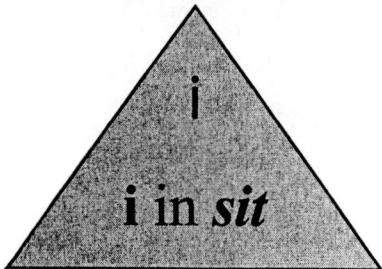

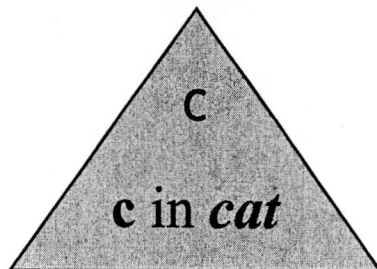

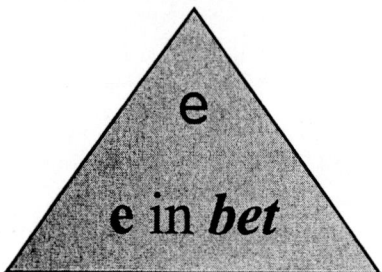

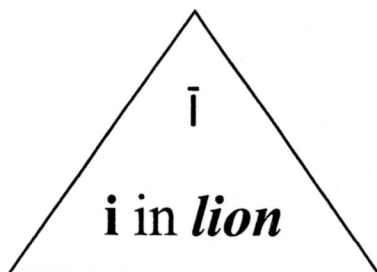

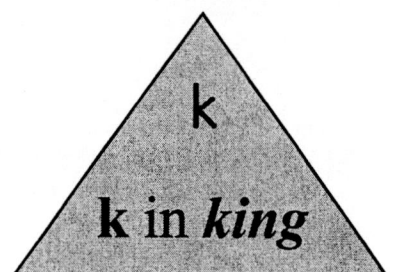

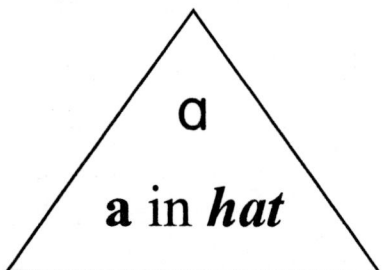

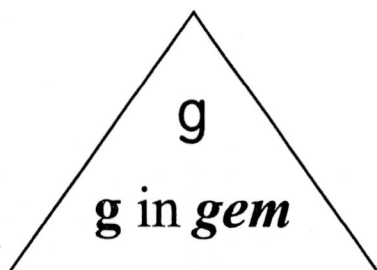

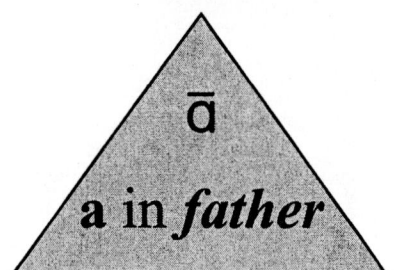

d
d in *dog*

l
l in *land*

ē
e in *feet*

i
i in *sit*

c
c in *cat*

f
f in *fan*

e
e in *bet*

ī
i in *lion*

k
k in *king*

a
a in *hat*

g
g in *gem*

ā
a in *father*

☐ I practiced my flashcards today.

M m

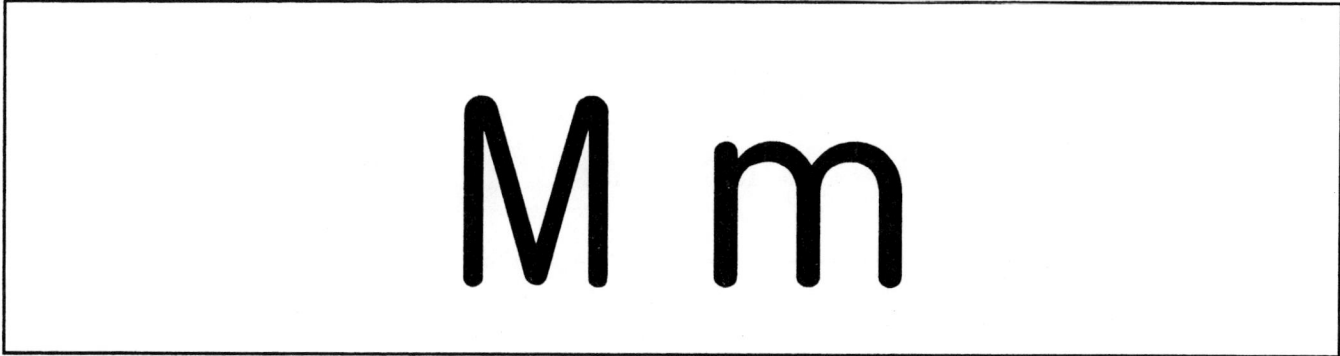

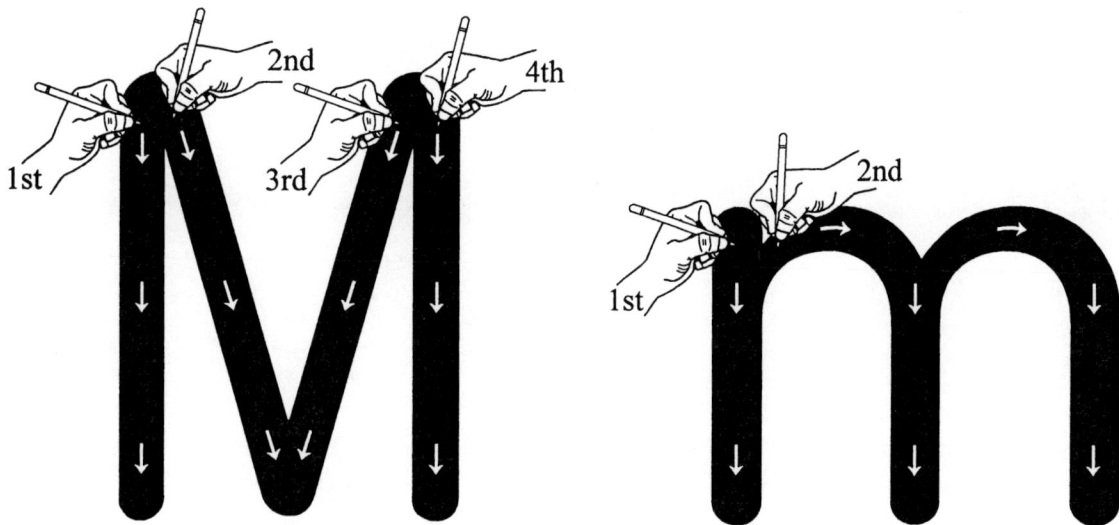

Write the letters across each line.
As you write them, say the sound of "**m**" in *man*.

M M M M M

m m m m m

☐ I practiced my flashcards today.
(Remember to add this new card to your flashcards.)

REMEMBER!
M or m sounds like **m** in *man*.

Put a *circle* on the words that have the Latin ɑ sound.*
Put a *box* on the words that have the Latin e sound.
Put a *triangle* on the words that have the Latin i sound.

bite

slept

hay

△ trip

○ away

○ soda

bee

rake

□ leg

□ ten

△ thing

○ camel

□ get

sat

game

△ list

tight

cat

△ tip

○ giant

angel

△ miss

reap

meet

□ wet

way

sad

*Careful! It may not be the English "a" that makes the Latin "ɑ" sound.

☐ I practiced my flashcards today.

Latin Workbook - Level 1
Copyright © 1996 by Karen Mohs

N n

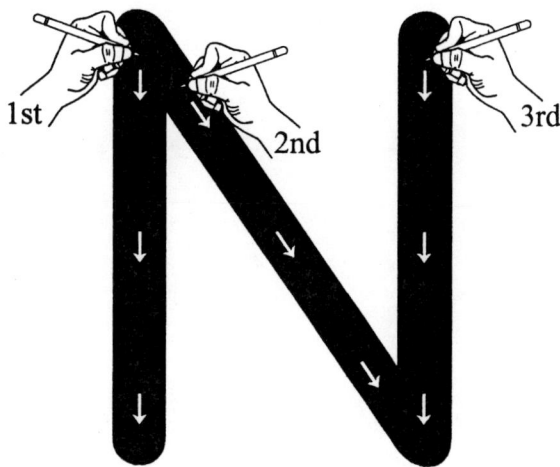

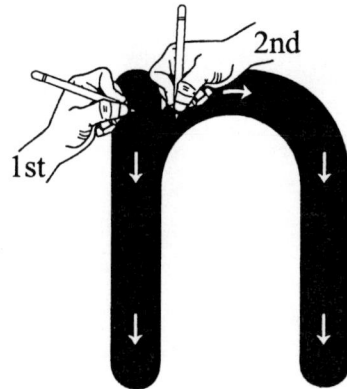

Write the letters across each line.
As you write them, say the sound of **"n"** in *nut*.

N N N N N

n n n n n

☐ I practiced my flashcards today.
(Remember to add this new card to your flashcards.)

Match the Latin letters with their sounds.

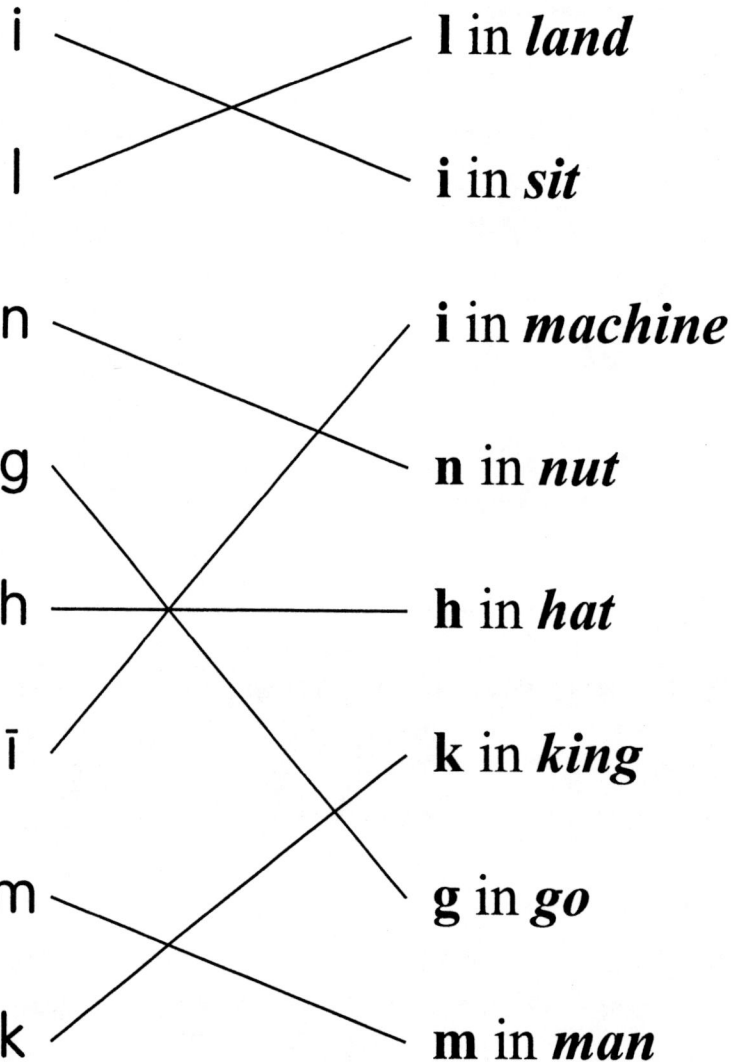

i   **l** in *land*

l   **i** in *sit*

n   **i** in *machine*

g   **n** in *nut*

h   **h** in *hat*

ī   **k** in *king*

m   **g** in *go*

k   **m** in *man*

☐ I practiced my flashcards today.

Latin Workbook - Level 1
Copyright © 1996 by Karen Mohs

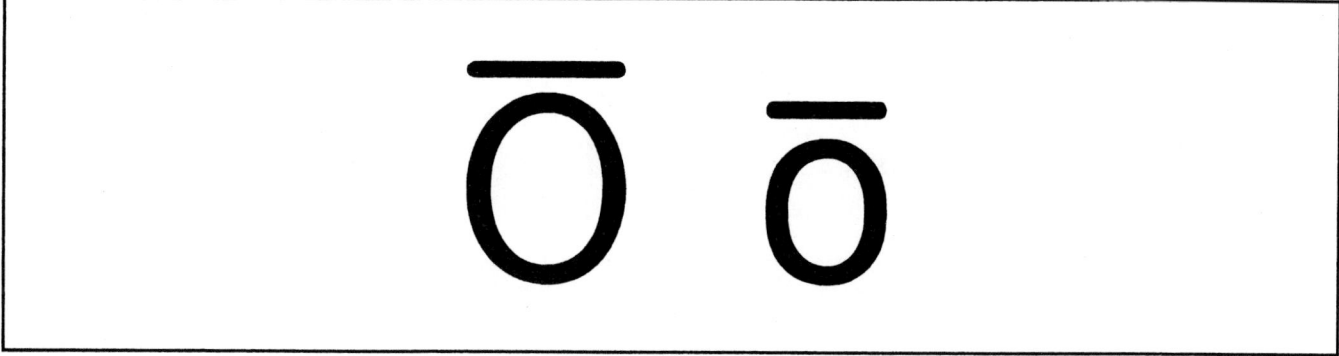

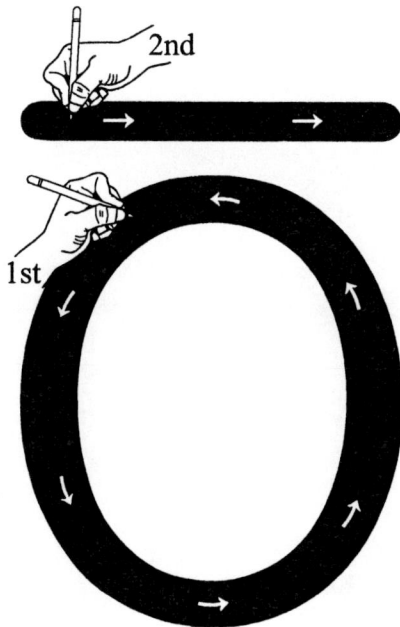

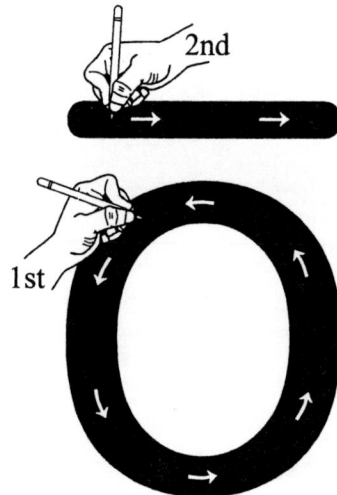

Write the letters across each line.
As you write them, say the sound of "**o**" in *note*.

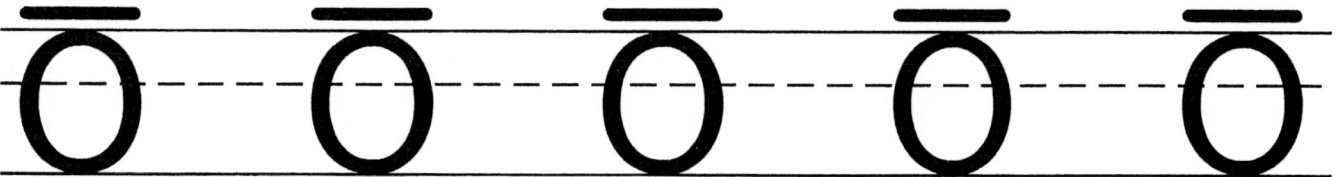

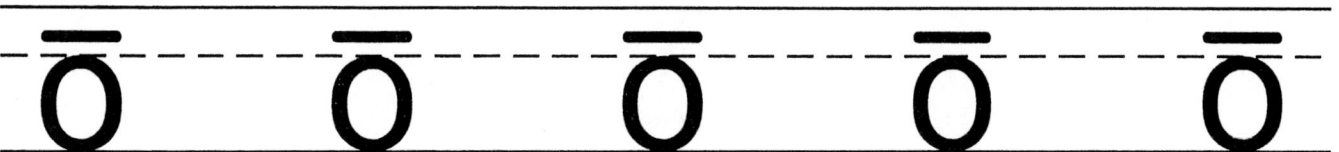

☐ I practiced my flashcards today.
(Remember to add this new card to your flashcards.)

Fill in the blanks with the missing lowercase Latin letters.

1. Latin **m** sounds like the **m** in *man*.

2. Latin **k** sounds like the **k** in *king*.

3. Latin **i** sounds like the **i** in *sit*.

4. Latin **l** sounds like the **l** in *land*.

5. Latin **ō** sounds like the **o** in *note*.

6. Latin **n** sounds like the **n** in *nut*.

☐ I practiced my flashcards today.

O o

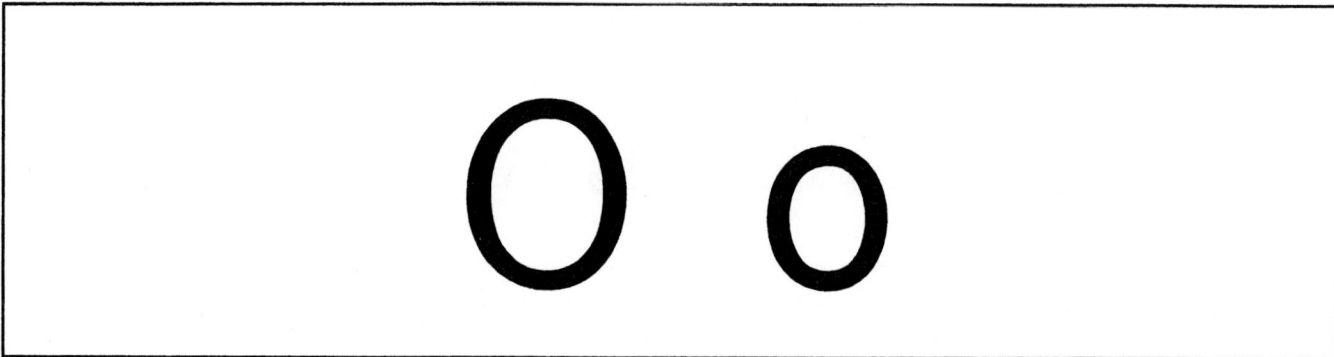

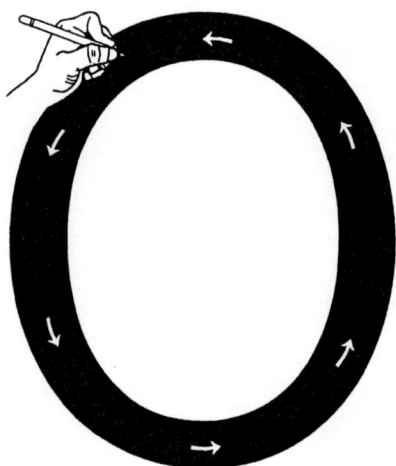

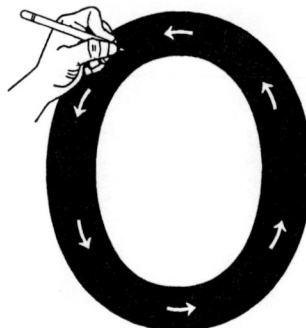

Write the letters across each line.
As you write them, say the sound of "o" in *omit*.

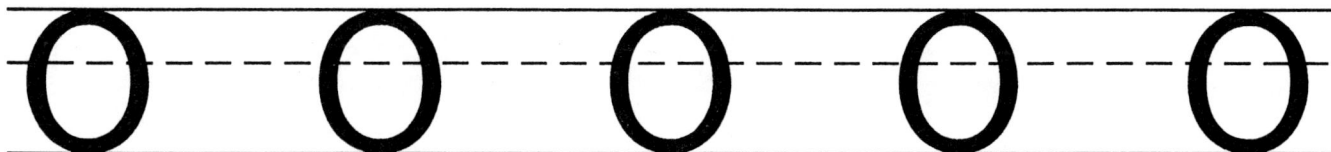

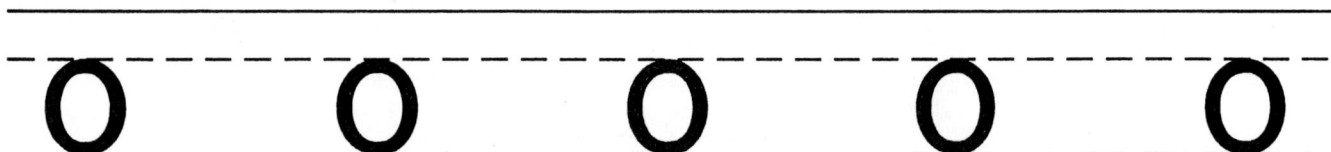

O   O   O   O   O

O   O   O   O   O

☐   I practiced my flashcards today.
(Remember to add this new card to your flashcards.)

Write the words under the correct Latin sounds.

obey	bone	omit	float
omega	bowl	roast	okay

ō

o

bone

obey

bowl

omega

roast

omit

float

okay

*Both Latin "o" sounds are "long." The ō as in *note* is held longer than the o as in *omit.*

☐ I practiced my flashcards today.

Latin Workbook - Level 1
Copyright © 1996 by Karen Mohs

P p

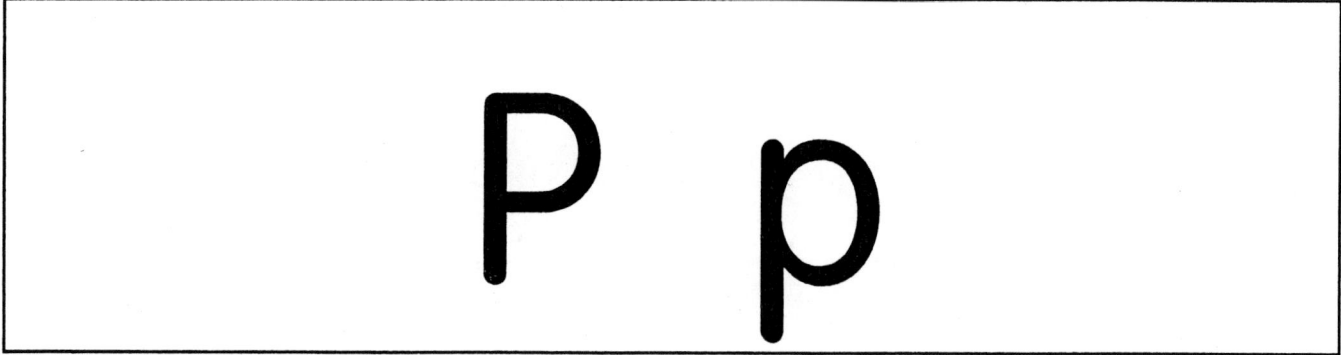

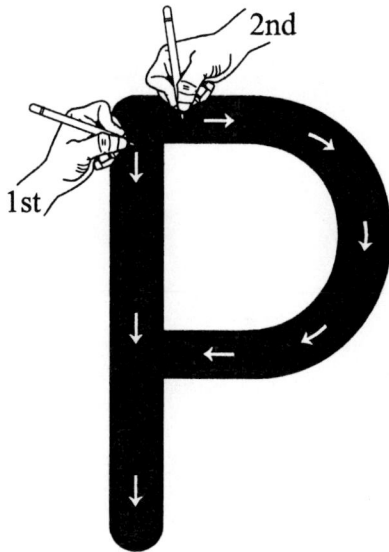

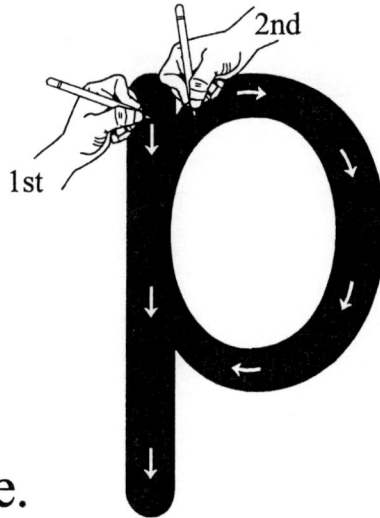

Write the letters across each line.
As you write them, say the sound of "**p**" in *pit*.

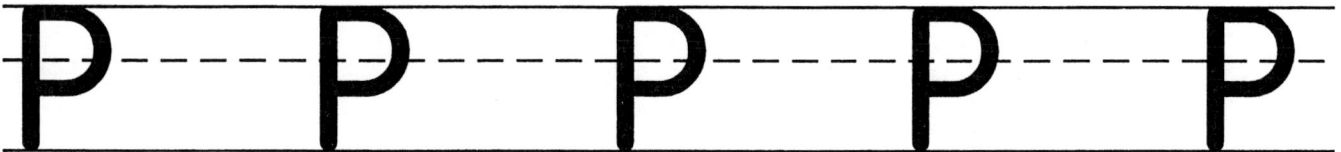

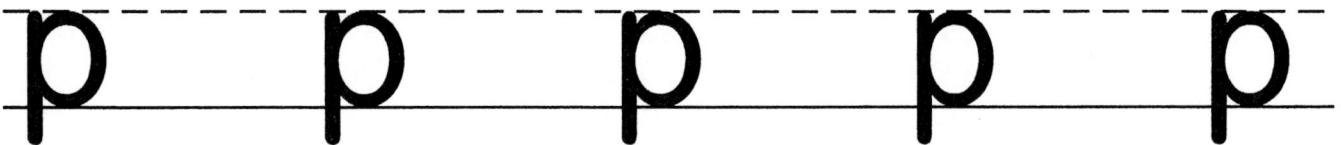

P   P   P   P   P

p   p   p   p   p

☐ I practiced my flashcards today.
(Remember to add this new card to your flashcards.)

REMEMBER!
P or p sounds like **p** in *pit*.

Circle *yes* if the sentence is true. Circle *no* if it is not true.

yes *no*   1. The Latin letter ᴍ sounds like the **m** in *mice*.

yes *no*   2. The Latin letter ᴘ sounds like the **p** in *pan*.

yes *no*   3. The Latin letter ᴏ sounds like the **o** in *hot*.

yes *no*   4. The Latin letter ᴄ sounds like the **c** in *ocean*.

yes *no*   5. The Latin letter ɴ sounds like the **n** in *napkin*.

yes *no*   6. The Latin letter ō sounds like the **o** in *rob*.

☐   I practiced my flashcards today.

Latin Workbook - Level 1
Copyright © 1996 by Karen Mohs

Q q

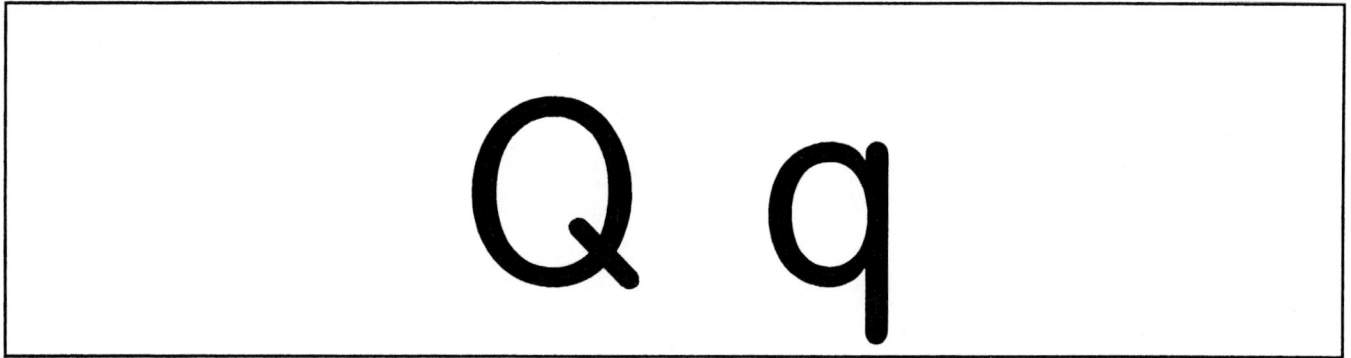

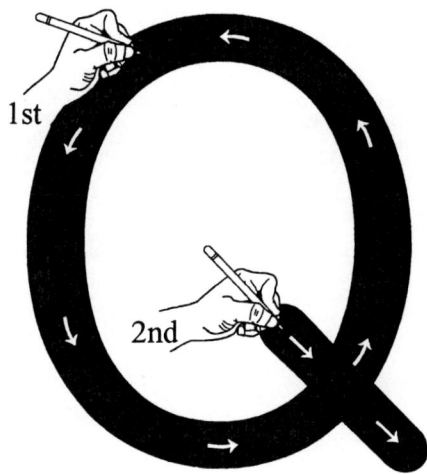

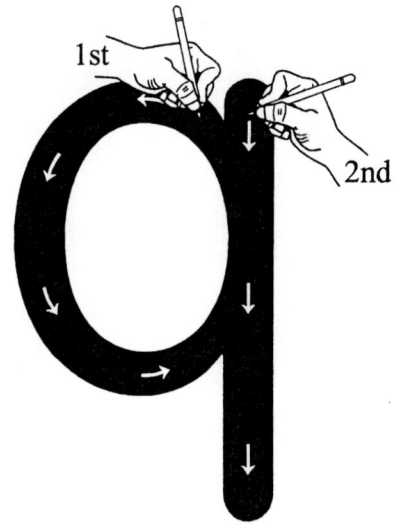

Write the letters across each line.
As you write them, say the sound of **"qu"** in *quit*.

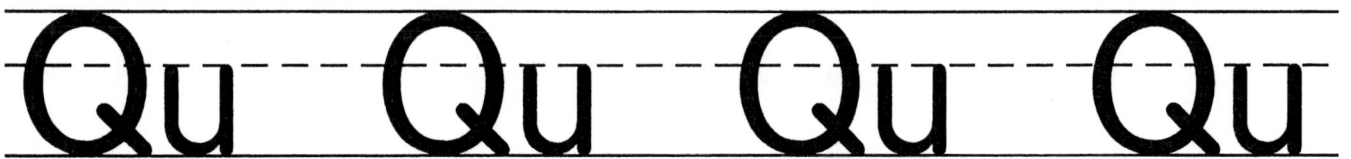

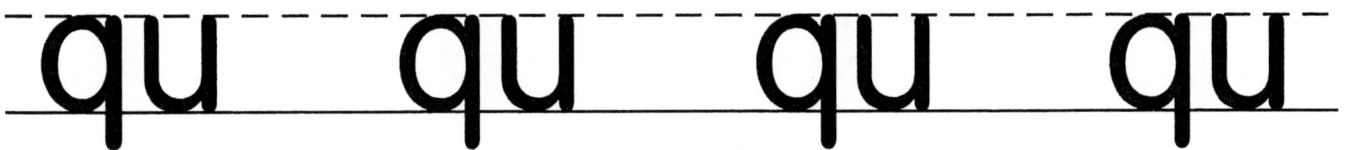

Qu Qu Qu Qu

qu qu qu qu

☐ I practiced my flashcards today.
(Remember to add this new card to your flashcards.)

REMEMBER!
Qu or qu sounds like **qu** in *quit*.

Draw a stem from each flower to its vase.

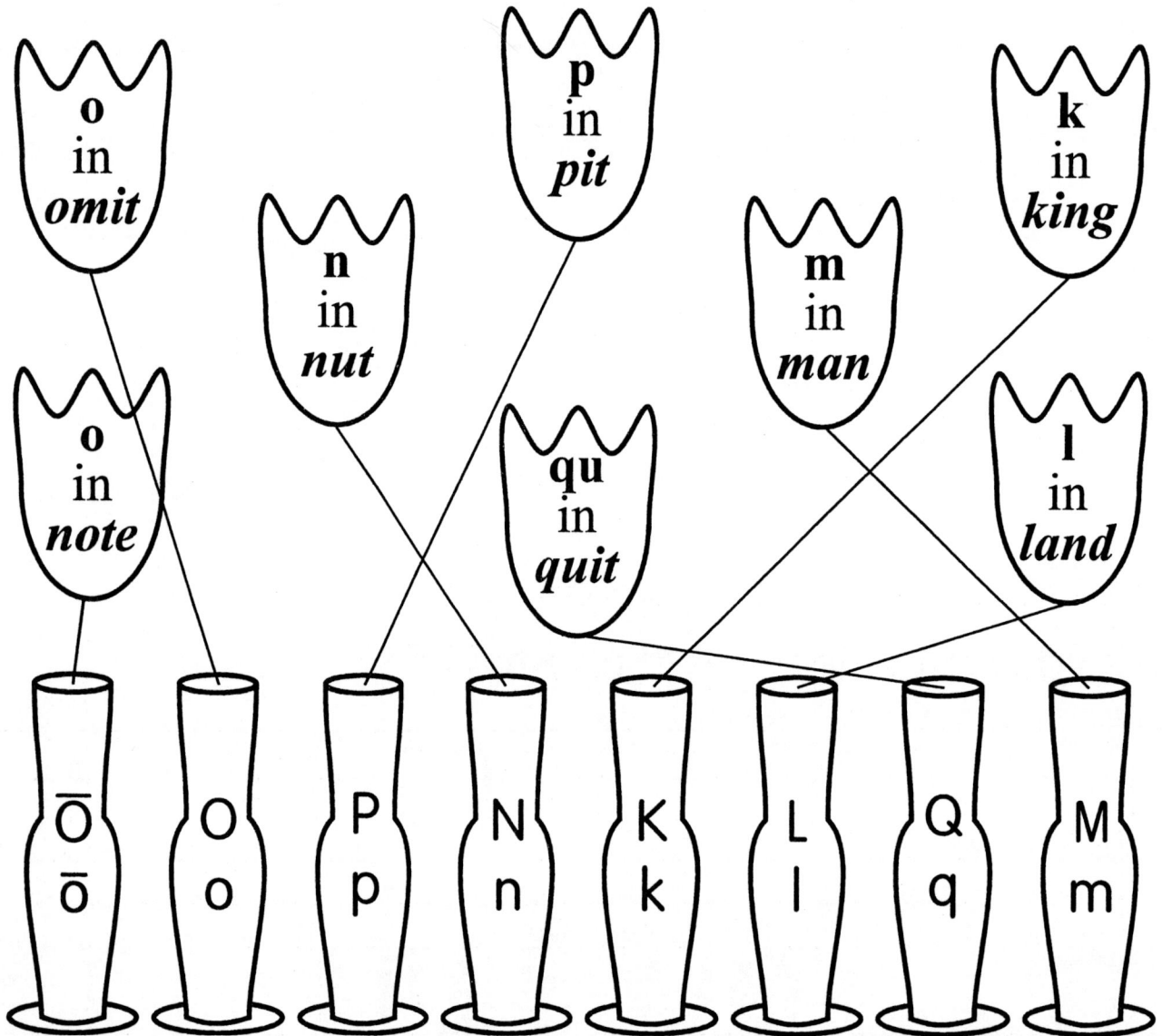

o
in
omit

o
in
note

n
in
nut

p
in
pit

qu
in
quit

m
in
man

k
in
king

l
in
land

Ō
ō

O
o

P
p

N
n

K
k

L
l

Q
q

M
m

☐ I practiced my flashcards today.

Latin Workbook - Level 1
Copyright © 1996 by Karen Mohs

R r

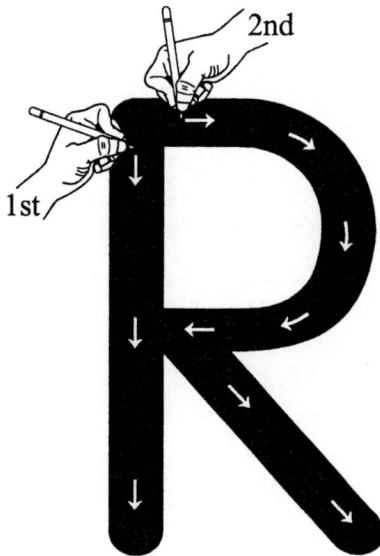

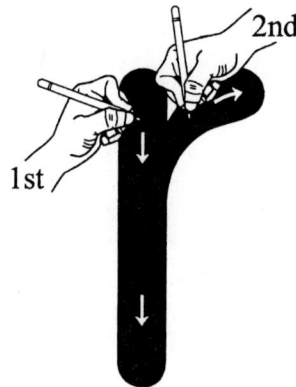

Write the letters across each line.
As you write them, say the sound of **"r"** in *run*.

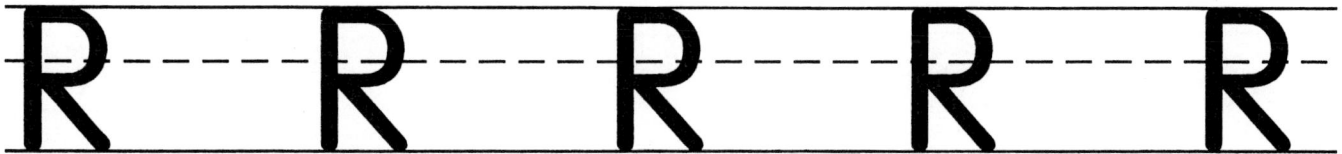

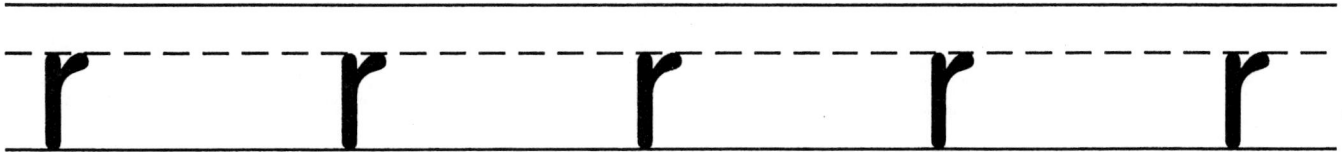

R R R R R

r r r r r

☐ I practiced my flashcards today.
(Remember to add this new card to your flashcards.)

REMEMBER!
R or r sounds like **r** in *run*.

Circle the correct Latin letter below each sound.

o in *note*	i in *machine*	m in *man*
(ō) o	(ī) i	n (m)
ey in *obey*	**c** in *cat*	**e** in *bet*
(ē) e	(c) q	ē (e)
r in *run*	**a** in *father*	**p** in *pit*
v (r)	(ā) a	(p) q
n in *nut*	**qu** in *quit*	**k** in *king*
(n) m	c (qu)	(k) qu
o in *omit*	**i** in *sit*	**a** in *idea*
ō (o)	ī (i)	ā (a)

☐ I practiced my flashcards today.

Latin Workbook - Level 1
Copyright © 1996 by Karen Mohs

S s

Write the letters across each line.
As you write them, say the sound of "**s**" in *sit*.

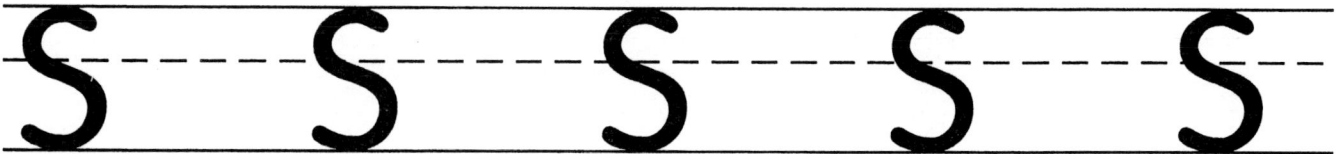

S   S   S   S   S

S   S   S   S   S

☐ I practiced my flashcards today.
(Remember to add this new card to your flashcards.)

Look at the Latin letter in the corner of the box.
Circle the words that have the sound it makes.

o	vote (okay) (Ohio) boot (omit)	s	easy (century) tease (sash) (salt)
c	(cable) face (cattle) (cream) race	ō	(hope) mop (grow) (cone) root
r	when five (argue) (barrel) (rat)	ē	eye (table) (day) (baby) eat

☐ I practiced my flashcards today.

T t

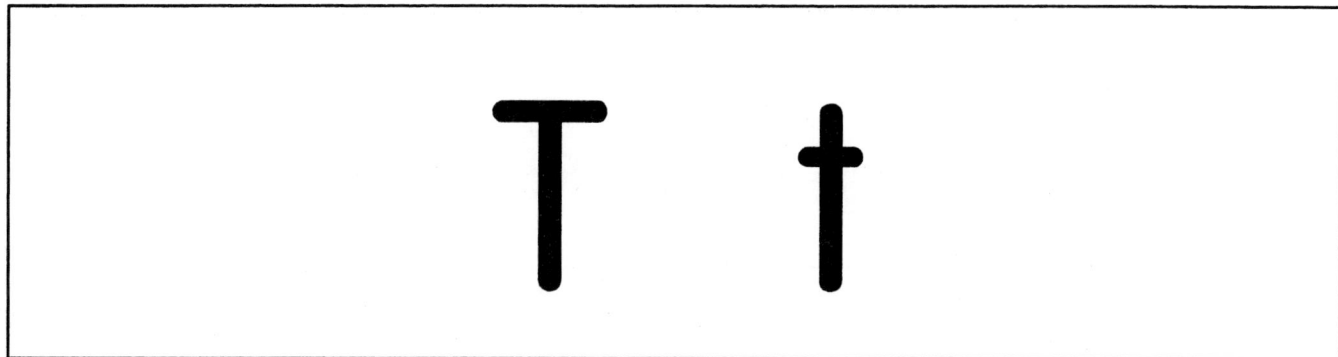

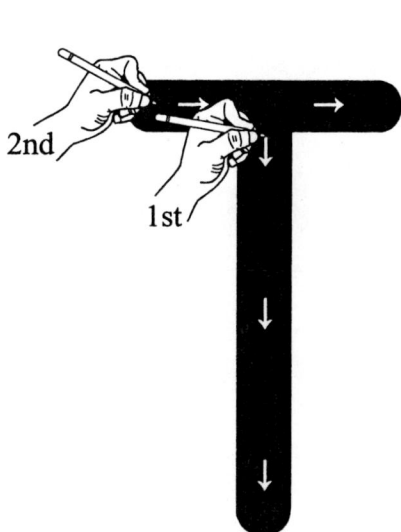

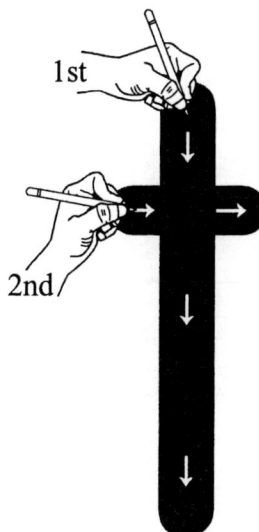

Write the letters across each line.
As you write them, say the sound of "t" in *tag*.

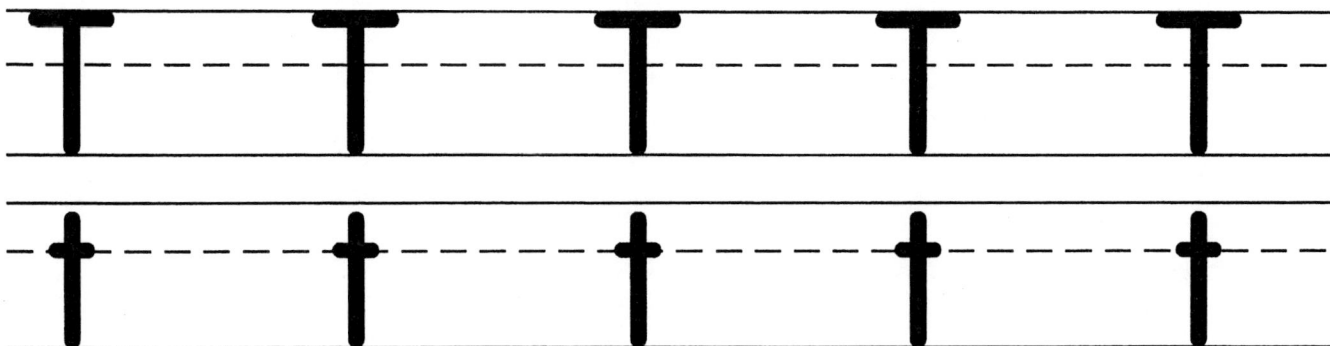

□ I practiced my flashcards today.
(Remember to add this new card to your flashcards.)

REMEMBER!
T or t sounds like **t** in *tag*.

Circle the words that have the sound of the Latin letters at the beginning of the row.

s	can (sat)	days (yes)	(less) fuse
t	(tag) the	(mat) (treat)	thank thing
ō	fox (roam)	(toast) often	omit (bold)
p	graph phone	(pie) (apple)	(scrap) rack
o	(obey) (okay)	goat hog	frog (oasis)

☐ I practiced my flashcards today.

Ū ū

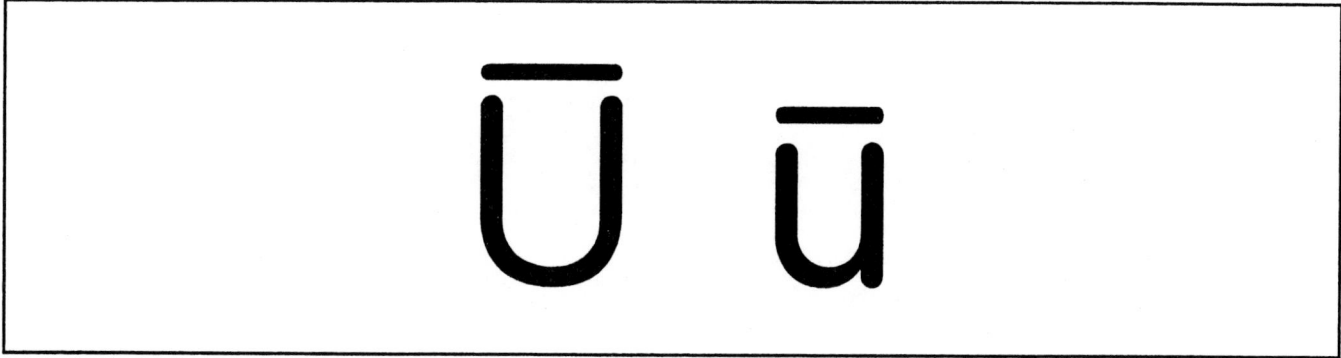

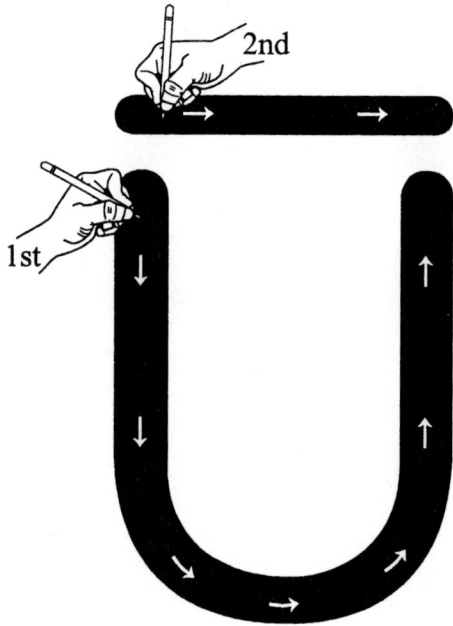

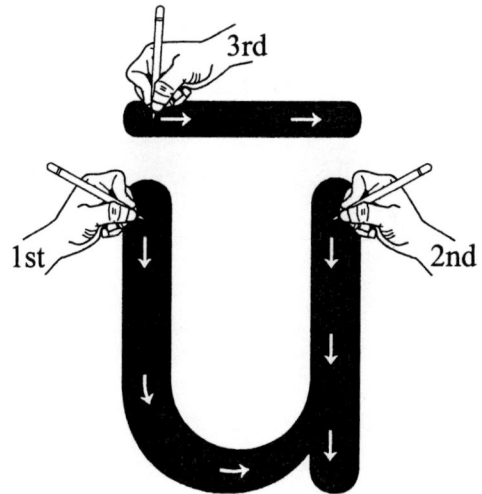

Write the letters across each line.
As you write them, say the sound of "**u**" in *rule*.

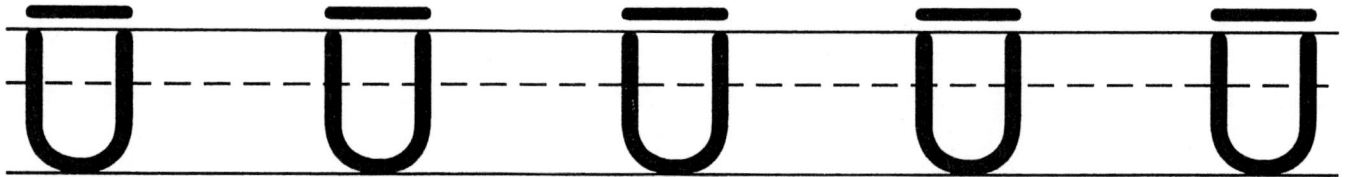

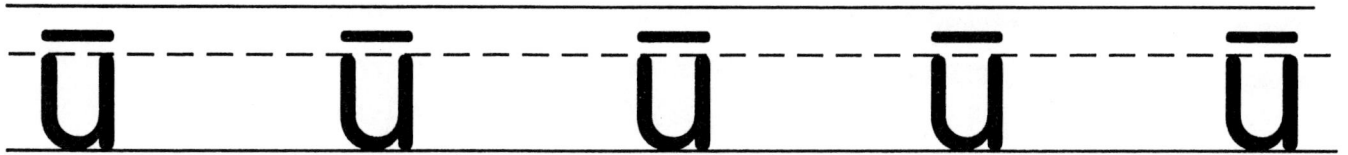

Fill in the blanks with the missing lowercase Latin letters.

1. Latin ___p___ sounds like the **p** in *pit*.

2. Latin ___s___ sounds like the **s** in *sit*.

3. Latin ___t___ sounds like the **t** in *tag*.

4. Latin ___qu___ sounds like the **qu** in *quit*.

5. Latin ___u̅___ sounds like the **u** in *rule*.

6. Latin ___r___ sounds like the **r** in *run*.

☐ I practiced my flashcards today.

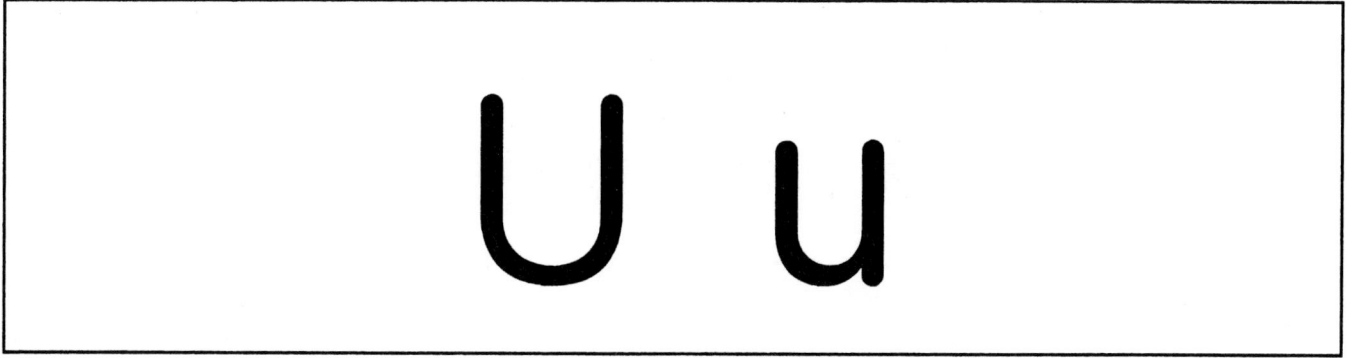

U u

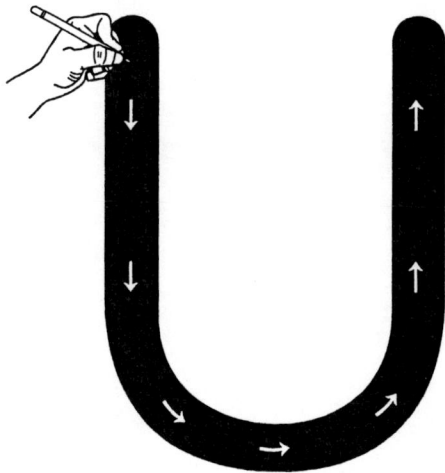

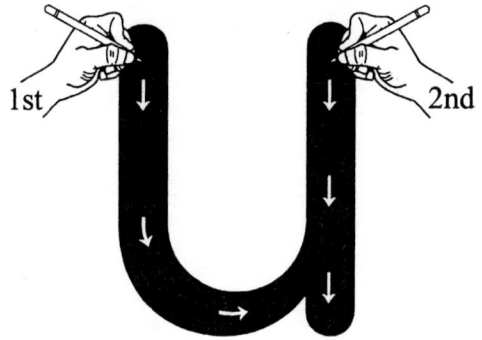

Write the letters across each line.
As you write them, say the sound of "**u**" in *put*.

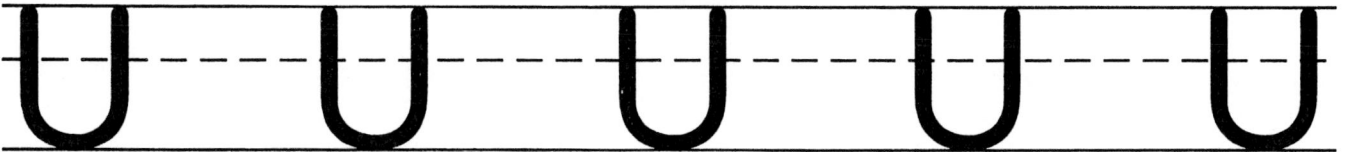

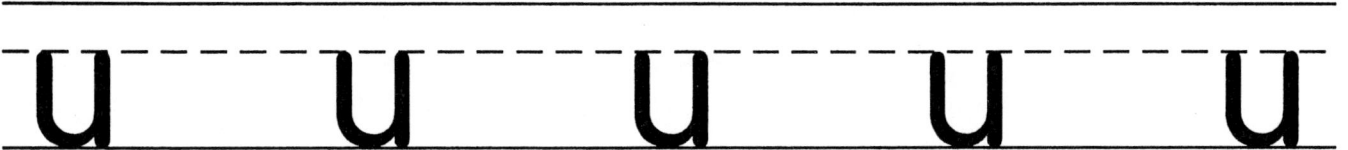

U   U   U   U   U

u   u   u   u   u

☐ I practiced my flashcards today.
(Remember to add this new card to your flashcards.)

Write the words under the correct Latin sounds.

| took | book | bloom | drool |
| boot | glue | lure | full |

ū

boot

bloom

drool

glue

u

took

book

lure

full

☐ I practiced my flashcards today.

V v

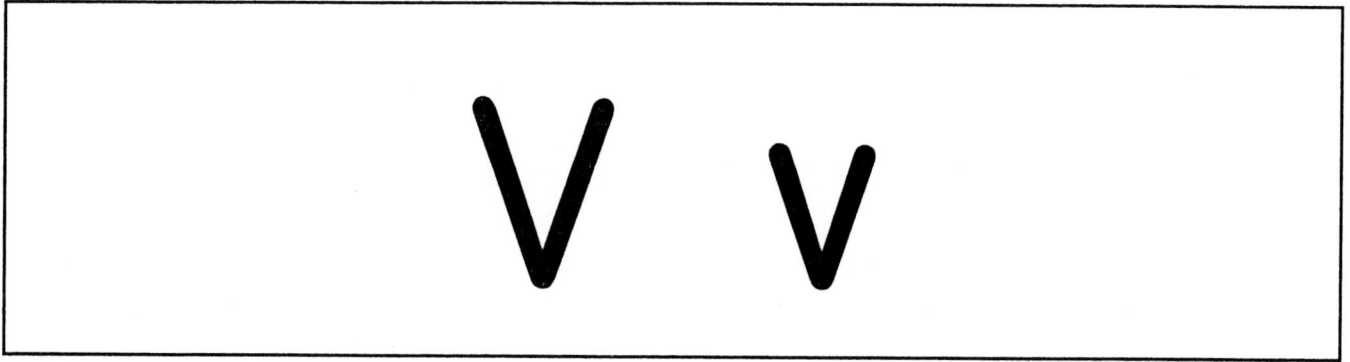

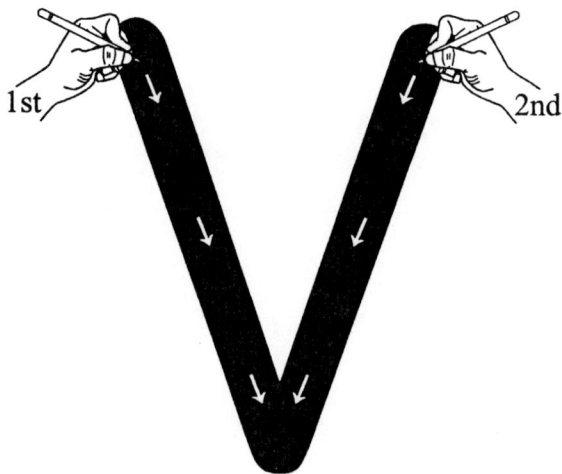

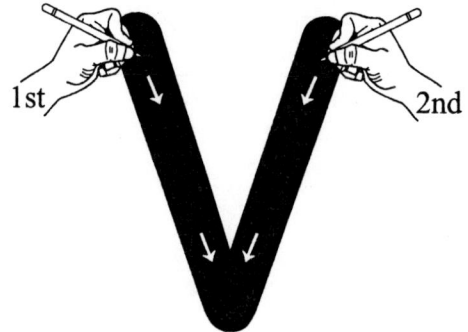

Write the letters across each line.
As you write them, say the sound of "**w**" in *way*.

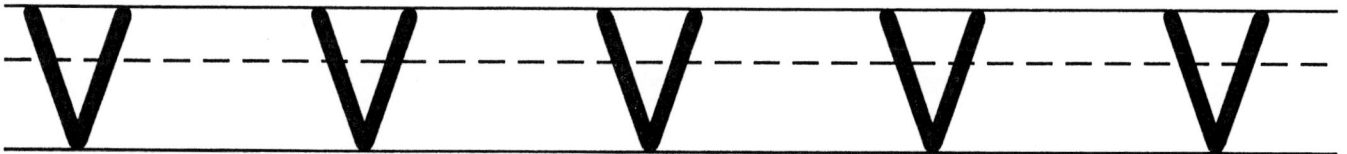

V V V V V

V V V V V

☐ I practiced my flashcards today.
(Remember to add this new card to your flashcards.)

Match the Latin letters with their sounds.

s   **r** in *run*

o   **u** in *rule*

r   **o** in *omit*

ū   **s** in *sit*

v   **o** in *note*

t   **w** in *way*

u   **t** in *tag*

ō   **u** in *put*

☐   I practiced my flashcards today.

X x

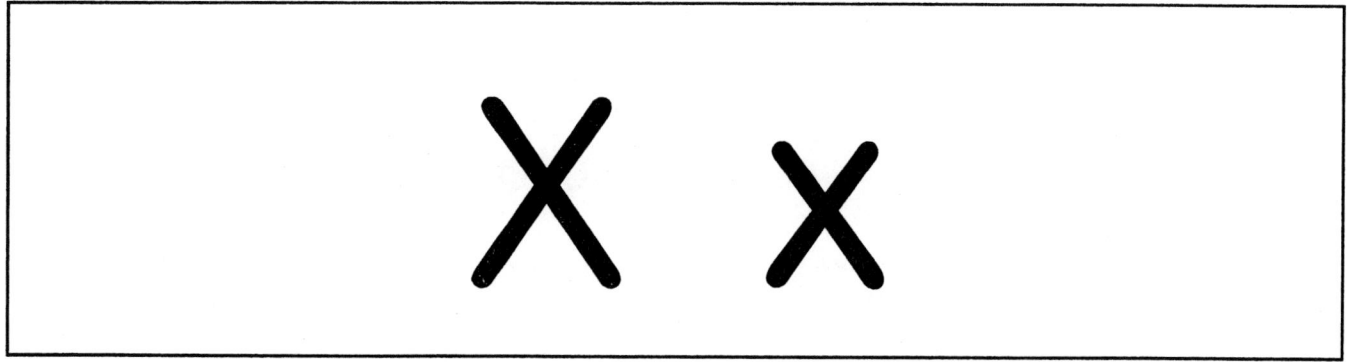

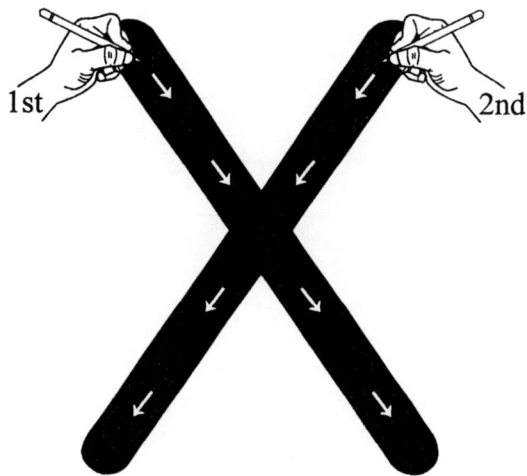

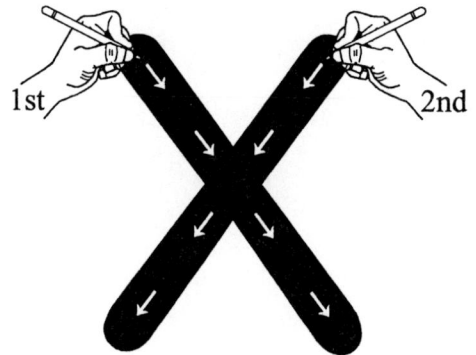

Write the letters across each line.
As you write them, say the sound of **"ks"** in *socks*.

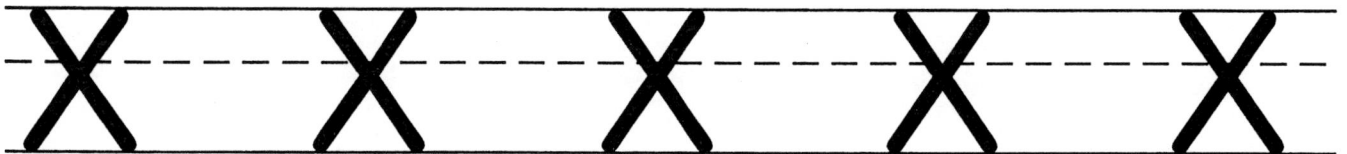

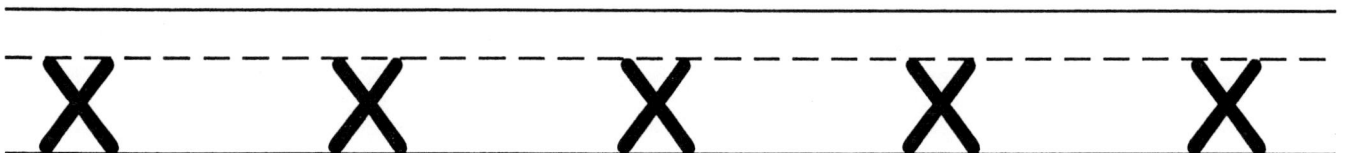

☐ I practiced my flashcards today.
(Remember to add this new card to your flashcards.)

Write the Latin letters for the first sound you hear in the English words.

English	Latin	English	Latin
art	ā	lamb	l
head	h	quick	qu
page	p	sing	s
win	v	gag	g
far	f	nest	n
ride	r	kite	k
map	m	table	t

☐ I practiced my flashcards today.

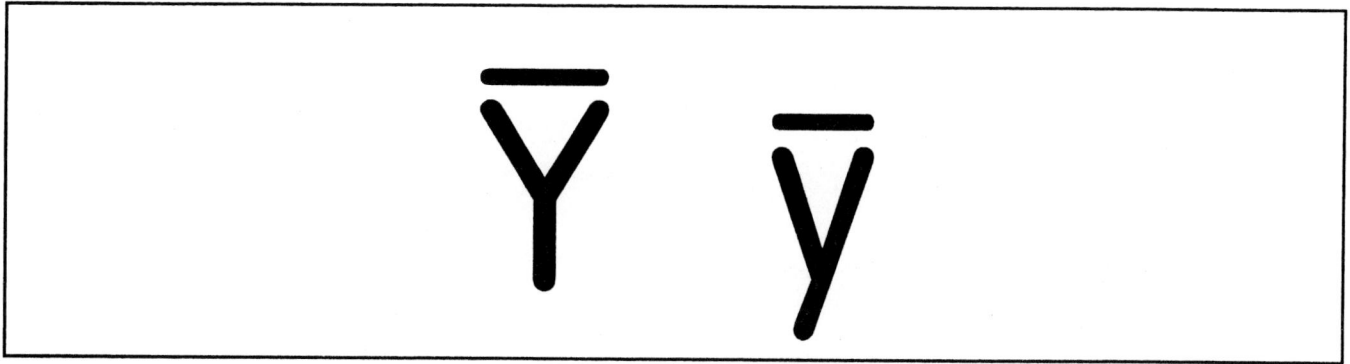

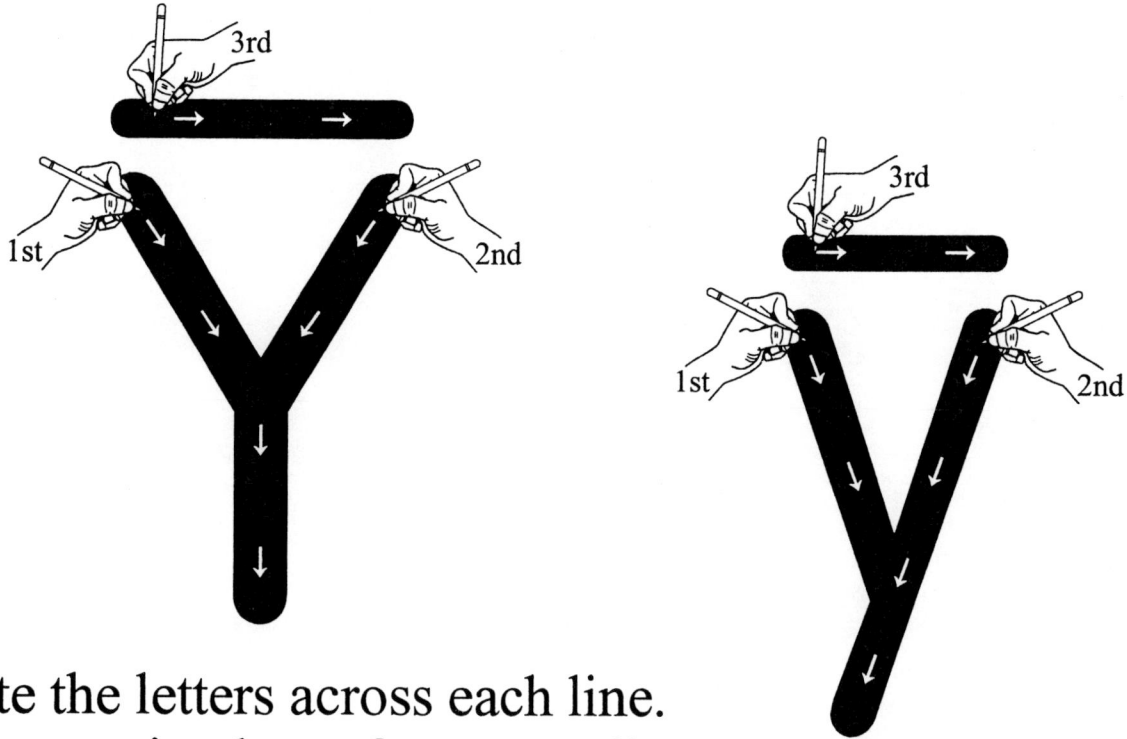

Write the letters across each line.
As you write them, form your lips to say **"oo"** but
say **"ee"** instead. (Hold the sound longer than Latin y.)

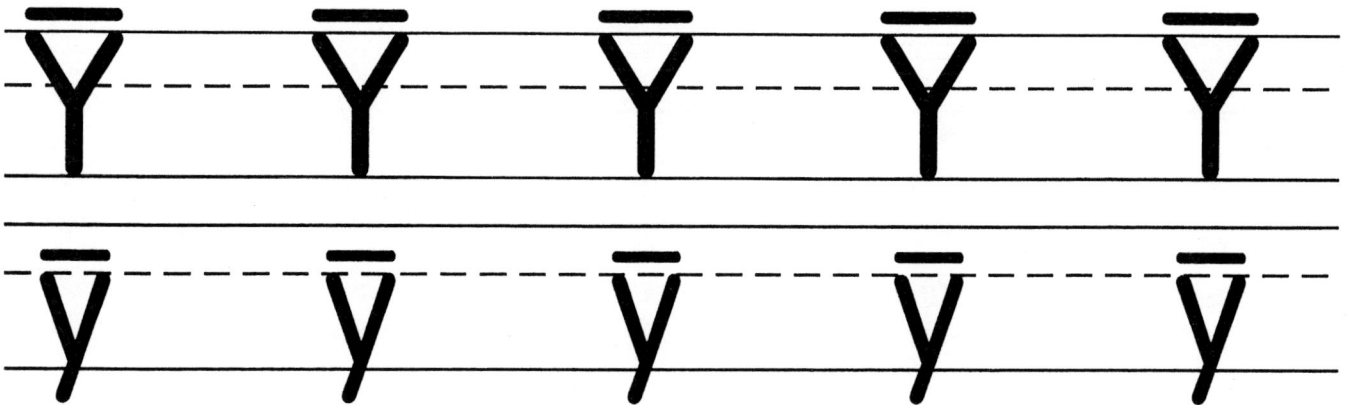

☐ I practiced my flashcards today.
(Remember to add this new card to your flashcards.)

Fill in the blanks with the missing lowercase Latin letters.

1. Latin ___t___ sounds like the **t** in *tag*.

2. Latin ___x___ sounds like the **ks** in *socks*.

3. Latin ___s___ sounds like the **s** in *sit*.

4. Latin ___v___ sounds like the **w** in *way*.

5. Latin ___ȳ___ sound is made by forming your
lips to say **oo** but saying **ee** instead.

6. Latin ___r___ sounds like the **r** in *run*.

☐ I practiced my flashcards today.

Y y

1st **2nd**

1st **2nd**

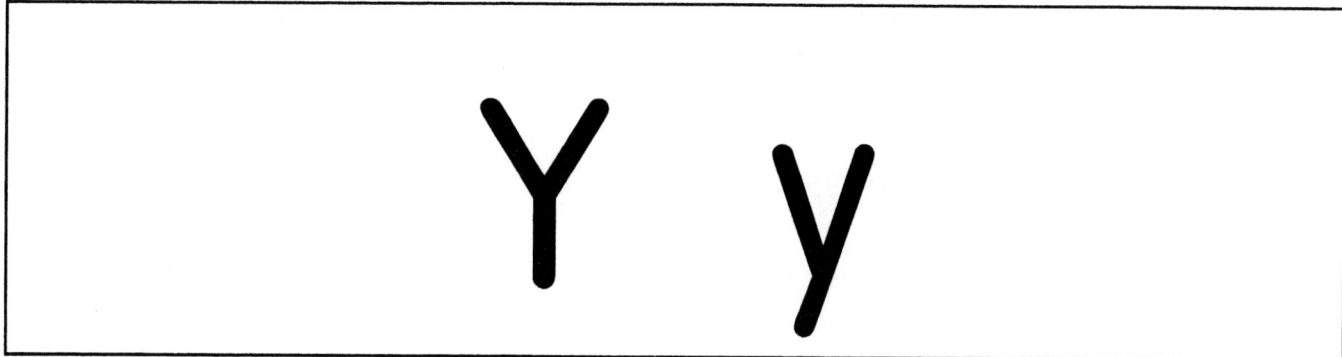

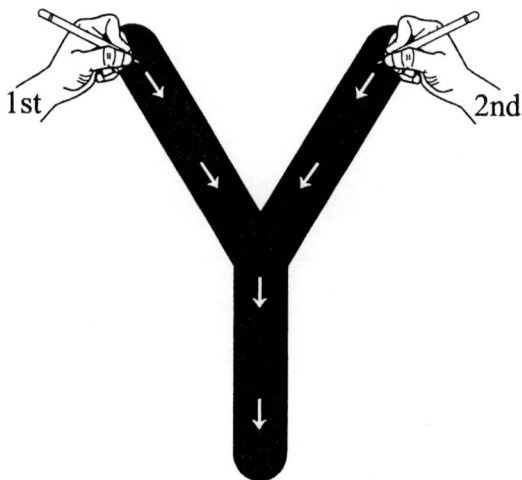

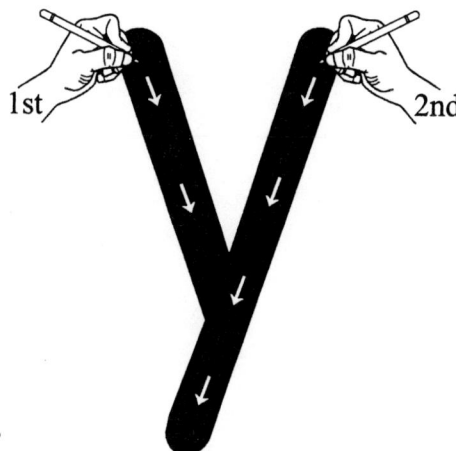

Write the letters across each line.
As you write them, form your lips to say **"oo"** but
say **"ee"** instead. (Hold the sound shorter than Latin ȳ.)

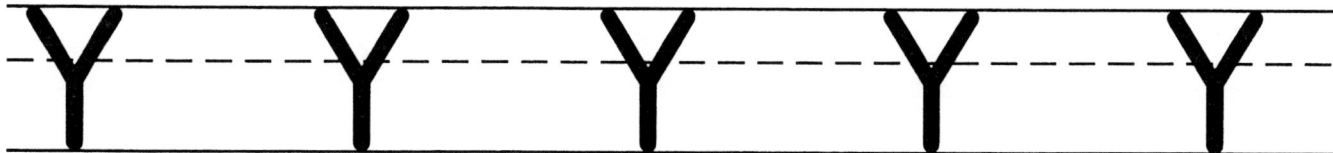

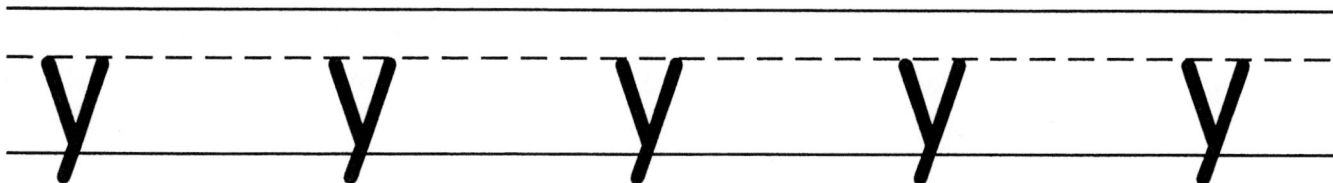

Y Y Y Y Y

y y y y y

☐ I practiced my flashcards today.
(Remember to add this new card to your flashcards.)

REMEMBER!
The Y or y sound is made when you
form your lips to say **oo** but say **ee** instead.
(Hold it shorter than Latin ȳ.)

Circle *yes* if the sentence is true. Circle *no* if it is not
true.

yes (*no*)　1.　The Latin letter **s** sounds like the **s** in *has*.

(*yes*)　*no*　2.　The Latin sound for ȳ is held longer than
　　　　　　　　the Latin sound for y.

yes (*no*)　3.　The Latin letter **v** sounds like the **v** in *very*.

yes (*no*)　4.　The Latin letter **g** sounds like the **g** in *age*.

yes (*no*)　5.　The Latin letter **c** sounds like the **c** in *ace*.

yes (*no*)　6.　The Latin letter **e** sounds like the **e** in *bee*.

☐　I practiced my flashcards today.

Latin Workbook - Level 1
Copyright © 1996 by Karen Mohs

Z z

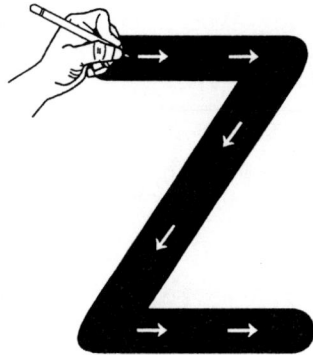

Write the letters across each line.
As you write them, say the sound of "**dz**" in *adze*.

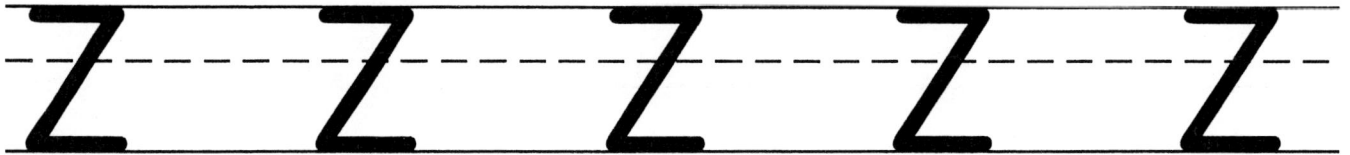

Z Z Z Z Z

Z Z Z Z Z

☐ I practiced my flashcards today.
(Remember to add this new card to your flashcards.)

REMEMBER!
Z or z sounds like **dz** in *adze*.

Circle the letters that match the sound in the big box.

u in *put*	ū	(u)	y
s in *sit*	(s)	c	z
p in *pit*	(p)	f	ph
dz in *adze*	k	x	(z)
o in *note*	(ō)	o	h
u in *rule*	(ū)	u	y
o in *omit*	ō	(o)	h
ks in *socks*	s	k	(x)
t in *tag*	th	f	(t)
w in *way*	(v)	r	u

☐ I practiced my flashcards today.

LET'S PRACTICE

Circle the words that have the sound of the letter in the big box.

v	(wash)	(west)	van
	(weed)	vast	ever
s	his	(same)	(bus)
	(miss)	busy	kids
ō	(hope)	rock	(over)
	bottle	(foam)	pot
g	(God)	gentle	gem
	age	(gas)	(get)
u	(look)	shout	(pull)
	hump	stool	(cookie)

☐ I practiced my flashcards today.

LET'S PRACTICE

Fill in the blanks with the missing sounds and words.

1. Latin v sounds like the __w__ in __way__.

2. Latin x sounds like the __ks__ in __socks__.

3. Latin u sounds like the __u__ in __put__.

4. Latin t sounds like the __t__ in __tag__.

5. Latin z sounds like the __dz__ in __adze__.

6. Latin ū sounds like the __u__ in __rule__.

☐ I practiced my flashcards today.

DIPHTHONGS

Latin has six diphthongs.

A diphthong combines two vowels to make one sound.

ɑe

sounds like

aye

Write the diphthong ɑe across each line.
As you write it, say the *"aye"* sound.

ɑe   ɑe   ɑe   ɑe

ɑe   ɑe   ɑe   ɑe

☐ I practiced my flashcards today.
(Remember to add this new card to your flashcards.)

Draw a line from the ɑe in the circle to the words with the Latin ɑe sound.

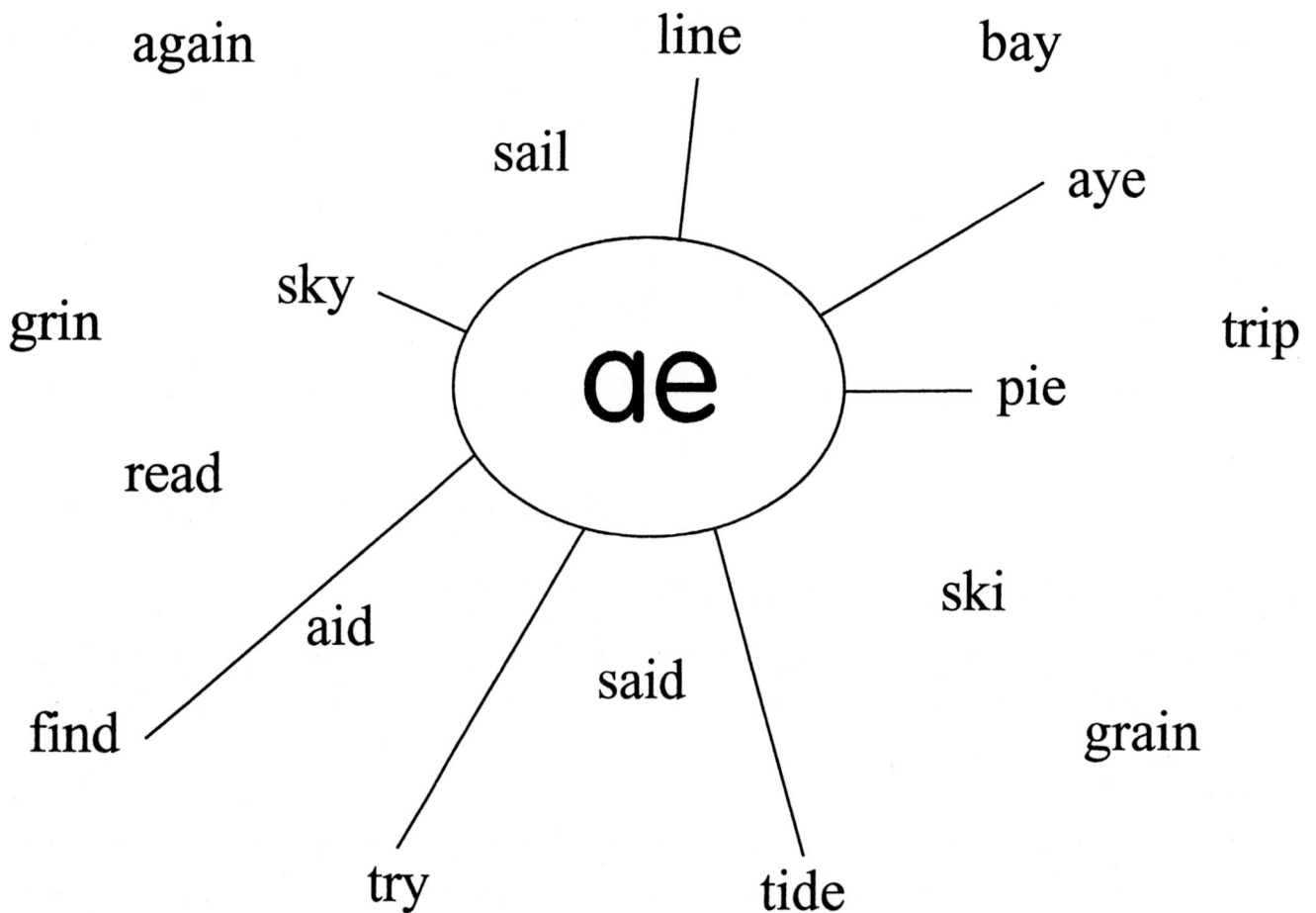

again

line

bay

sail

sky

aye

grin

ɑe

trip

pie

read

aid

ski

said

find

grain

try

tide

□ I practiced my flashcards today.

Latin Workbook - Level 1
Copyright © 1996 by Karen Mohs

DIPHTHONGS

Write the diphthong that makes the "*aye*" sound.

ae

au

sounds like
ow in *now*

Write the diphthong au across each line.
As you write it, say the "**ow**" sound in *now*.

au   au   au   au

au   au   au   au

☐ I practiced my flashcards today.
(Remember to add this new card to your flashcards.)

REMEMBER!
au sounds like **ow** in *now*.

Circle the word with the Latin sound.

ā	nap mane (ark)	s	has (miss) busy	o	often (obey) bone
g	age (game) engine	ē	(blade) set reed	au	know (cow) blow
ae	(try) say race	c	cent (cast) grace	i	(bit) high wide
z	zoo (adze) zero	v	(want) save vast	ū	bun (rude) mule

☐ I practiced my flashcards today.

66

DIPHTHONGS

Draw a line from each diphthong to its sound.

au   *aye*

ae   ow in *now*

ei

sounds like
ei in *neighbor*

Write the diphthong ei across each line.
As you write it, say the "**ei**" sound in *neighbor*.

ei   ei   ei   ei

ei   ei   ei   ei

☐ I practiced my flashcards today.
(Remember to add this new card to your flashcards.)

REMEMBER!
ei sounds like **ei** in *neighbor*.

Circle the correct Latin letter below each sound.

n in *nut*		ks in *socks*		ei in *neighbor*	
ȳ	(n)	(x)	k	ae	(ei)
w in *way*		**m** in *man*		**o** in *note*	
(v)	r	(m)	n	(ō)	o
r in *run*		**dz** in *adze*		**p** in *pit*	
t	(r)	x	(z)	(p)	q
aye		**u** in *put*		**s** in *sit*	
(ae)	ei	ū	(u)	(s)	c
t in *tag*		**qu** in *quit*		**ow** in *now*	
g	(t)	c	(qu)	(au)	av

☐ I practiced my flashcards today.

Latin Workbook - Level 1
Copyright © 1996 by Karen Mohs

DIPHTHONGS

Circle the correct diphthong for each sound.

ei in *neighbor*   au   ae   (ei)

ow in *now*   (au)   ae   ei

aye   au   (ae)   ei

eu

sounds like

ay-oo (in one syllable)

Write the diphthong eu across each line.
As you write it, say "***ay-oo***" as one syllable.

eu   eu   eu   eu

eu   eu   eu   eu

☐ I practiced my flashcards today.
(Remember to add this new card to your flashcards.)

Write the Latin letters that make the sound on each button.

Say
ay-oo
in one syllable.
∴

eu

Form your lips
to say *oo* but say
ee instead. Held longer.
∴

ȳ

Form your lips
to say *oo* but say
ee instead. Held shorter.
∴

y

Say
aye.
∴

ae

☐ I practiced my flashcards today.

DIPHTHONGS

Write the correct diphthong for each sound.

ay-oo eu   ei in *neighbor* ei

oe

sounds like
oy in *joy*

Write the diphthong oe across each line.
As you write it, say the "**oy**" sound in *joy*.

oe   oe   oe   oe   oe

oe   oe   oe   oe

☐ I practiced my flashcards today.
(Remember to add this new card to your flashcards.)

REMEMBER!
oe sounds like **oy** in *joy*.

Circle *yes* if the sentence is true. Circle *no* if it is not true.

(yes) no   1. The Latin letters ei sound like the **ei** in *eight*.

yes (no)   2. The Latin letters oe sound like the **oe** in *poet*.

yes (no)   3. The Latin letters au sound like the **ow** in *know*.

yes (no)   4. The Latin letters ae sound like the **ea** in *head*.

(yes) no   5. The Latin letters oe sound like the **oy** in *boy*.

(yes) no   6. The Latin letters eu sound like *ay-oo*.

☐   I practiced my flashcards today.

DIPHTHONGS

Draw a line from each diphthong to its sound.

ay-oo   oe
oy in ***joy***   ɑu
ow in ***now***   eu

ui

sounds like

uee in ***queen***

Write the diphthong ui across each line.
As you write it, say the "**uee**" sound in ***queen***.

ui   ui   ui   ui

ui   ui   ui   ui

☐ I practiced my flashcards today.
(Remember to add this new card to your flashcards.)

Circle the words that have the sound of the Latin letters at the beginning of the row.

oe	(toy) every	tray (boy)	(enjoy) grow
ui	(queen) equip	(weep) suit	ruin (sweep)
ae	(guy) head	say eat	(fly) (kite)
ei	(weigh) (eight)	either leaf	(rein) receive
au	below flow	(clown) (cloud)	(flower) glow

☐ I practiced my flashcards today.

LET'S PRACTICE

Circle the letters that match the sound in the big box.

ow in ***now***	ae	(au)	ei
	eu	oe	ui
aye	(ae)	au	ei
	eu	oe	ui
oy in ***joy***	ae	au	ei
	eu	(oe)	ui
uee in ***queen***	ae	au	ei
	eu	oe	(ui)
ay-oo	ae	au	ei
	(eu)	oe	ui

☐ I practiced my flashcards today.

LET'S PRACTICE

Fill in the blanks with the missing sounds and words.

1. Latin ui sounds like __uee__ in __queen__.

2. Latin eu sounds like __ay-oo__.

3. Latin oe sounds like __oy__ in __joy__.

4. Latin au sounds like __ow__ in __now__.

5. Latin ei sounds like __ei__ in __neighbor__.

6. Latin ae sounds like __aye__.

☐ I practiced my flashcards today.

SPECIAL CONSONANTS

Most Latin consonants sound like the same English consonants, but some have special sounds.

bs

sounds like

ps

Write the consonants bs across each line.
As you write them, say the "*ps*" sound.

bs   bs   bs   bs

bs   bs   bs   bs

☐ I practiced my flashcards today.
(Remember to add this new card to your flashcards.)

Circle the words that have the sound of the Latin letters at the beginning of the row.

s	his	(cross)	(soup)
oe	(royal)	sow	may
ei	side	pie	(reign)
v	(want)	vote	(wish)
ū	(shoot)	(room)	plum
ae	day	have	(lie)
bs	ads	(lips)	slabs
au	saw	claw	(down)
g	(gust)	(ago)	gem
ui	quiz	(queen)	(weed)
u	(push)	trust	(butch)

☐ I practiced my flashcards today.

SPECIAL CONSONANTS

Write the Latin consonants that make the "*ps*" sound.

bs

bt

sounds like

pt

Write the consonants bt across each line.
As you write them, say the "*pt*" sound.

bt   bt   bt   bt

bt   bt   bt   bt

☐ I practiced my flashcards today.
(Remember to add this new card to your flashcards.)

REMEMBER!
bt sounds like *pt.*

Circle the letters that match the sound in the big box.

ay-oo	ui	ue	(eu)
ks in *socks*	s	(x)	k
uee in *queen*	(ui)	eu	ee
w in *way*	(v)	r	y
ei in *neighbor*	oa	ie	(ei)
sounds like *pt*	dt	(bt)	tb
ow in *now*	(au)	ov	av
aye	ai	(ae)	ei
sounds like *ps*	sp	ps	(bs)
oy in *joy*	eo	(oe)	eu

☐ I practiced my flashcards today.

SPECIAL CONSONANTS

Draw a line from the special consonants to their sounds.

bt ——————— *pt*

bs ——————— *ps*

ch

sounds like

ch in *character*

Write the consonants ch across each line.

As you write them, say the "**ch**" sound in *character*.

ch   ch   ch   ch

ch   ch   ch   ch

☐ I practiced my flashcards today.
(Remember to add this new card to your flashcards.)

REMEMBER!
ch sounds like **ch** in *character*.

Circle the word with the Latin sound.

c	brace (cane) rice	oe	toe poet (boil)	e	(net) feet thing
bs	(hips) absent cabs	ae	greed (slide) bay	g	stage gem (guess)
v	vat ever (wing)	ui	quest (tweed) build	ch	(arc) chart arch
bt	debt (apt) table	au	toe low (loud)	ei	tie seige (vein)

☐ I practiced my flashcards today.

Latin Workbook - Level 1
Copyright © 1996 by Karen Mohs

SPECIAL CONSONANTS

Circle the correct special consonants for each sound.

ch	bs	bt	(ch)
pt	bs	(bt)	ch
ps	(bs)	bt	ch

gu
sounds like
gu in *anguish*

Write the consonants gu across each line.
As you write them, say the "**gu**" sound in *anguish*.

gu gu gu gu

gu gu gu gu

☐ I practiced my flashcards today.
(Remember to add this new card to your flashcards.)

Write the Latin letters for the first sound you hear in the English words.

sag	s	weep	ui
wish	v	tuck	t
Guam	gu	omit	o
owl	au	aye	ae
nick	n	mat	m
eight	ei	rush	r
pear	p	oil	oi

☐ I practiced my flashcards today.

SPECIAL CONSONANTS

Write the special consonants for each sound.

pt __bt__   *ps* __bs__

i

sounds like
y in *youth*

Write the consonant i across each line.
As you write it, say the "**y**" sound in *youth*.

i   i   i   i   i

i   i   i   i   i

☐ I practiced my flashcards today.
(Remember to add this new card to your flashcards.)

Fill in the blanks with the missing lowercase Latin letters.

1. Latin __gu__ sounds like the **gu** in *anguish*.

2. Latin __bt__ has the *pt* sound.

3. Latin __ch__ sounds like the **ch** in *character*.

4. Latin __ui__ sounds like the **uee** in *queen*.

5. Latin __i__ , used as a consonant, sounds like the **y** in *youth*.

6. Latin __bs__ has the *ps* sound.

☐ I practiced my flashcards today.

SPECIAL CONSONANTS

Draw a line from each special consonant to its sound.

gu in *anguish* —————— gu

y in *youth* ———— ch

ch in *character* ———— i

ph

sounds like

ph in *phone*

Write the consonants ph across each line.
As you write them, say the "**ph**" sound in *phone*.

ph   ph   ph   ph

ph   ph   ph   ph

☐ I practiced my flashcards today.
(Remember to add this new card to your flashcards.)

REMEMBER!
ph sounds like **ph** in *phone*.

Draw a stem from each flower to its vase.

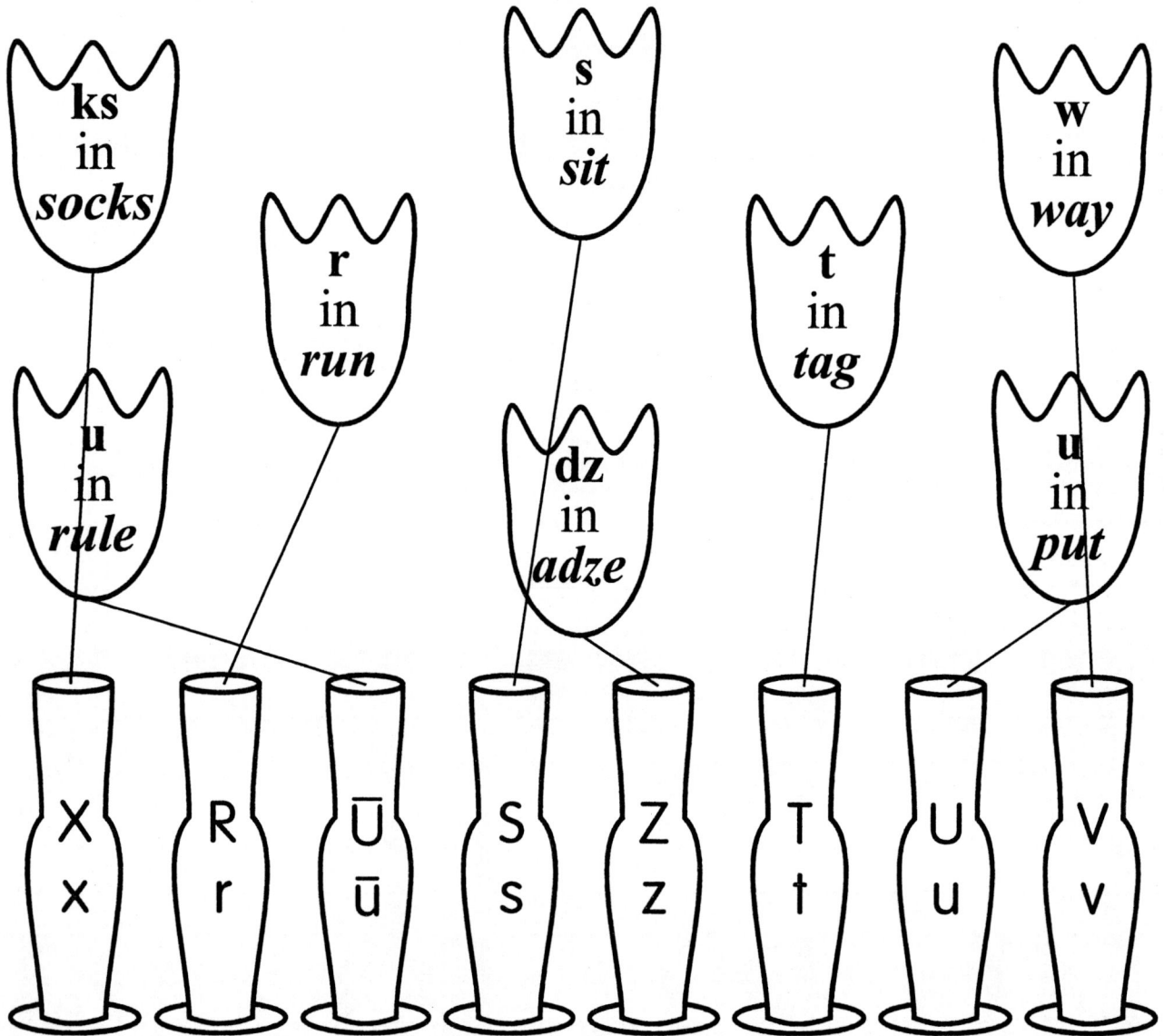

ks
in
socks

r
in
run

s
in
sit

w
in
way

t
in
tag

u
in
rule

dz
in
adze

u
in
put

X
x

R
r

Ū
ū

S
s

Z
z

T
t

U
u

V
v

☐ I practiced my flashcards today.

SPECIAL CONSONANTS

Circle the special consonants for each sound.

ps	[bs]	bt	ph
ph	bs	bt	[ph]
pt	bs	[bt]	ph

su

sounds like
su in *suave*

Write the letters su across each line.
As you write them, say the **"su"** sound in *suave*.

su su su su

su su su su

☐ I practiced my flashcards today.
(Remember to add this new card to your flashcards.)

Write the Latin letters that make the sound on each pie.

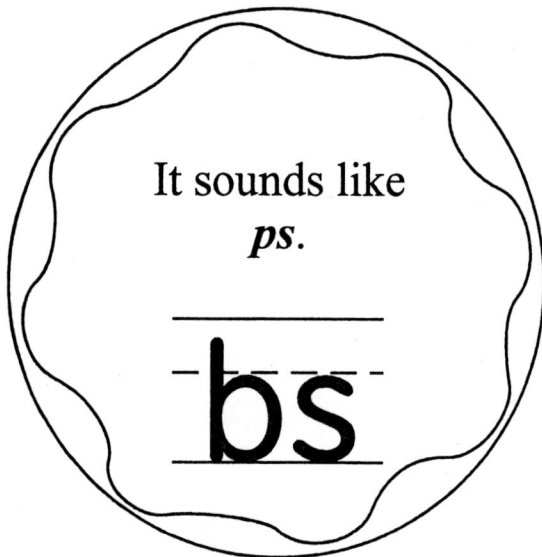

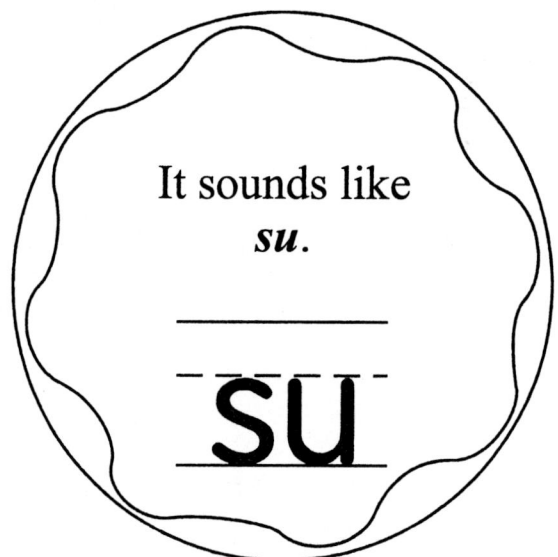

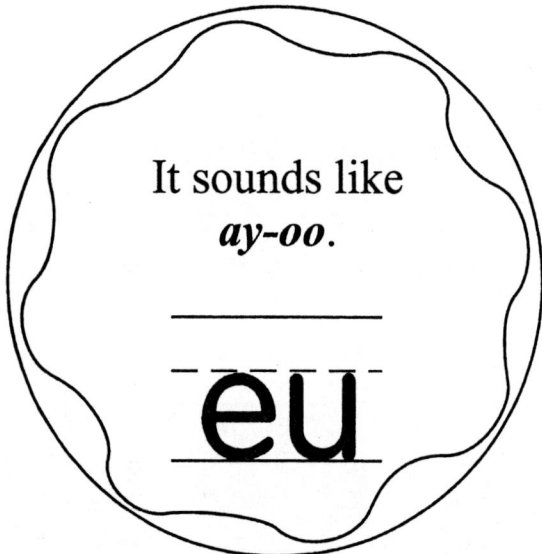

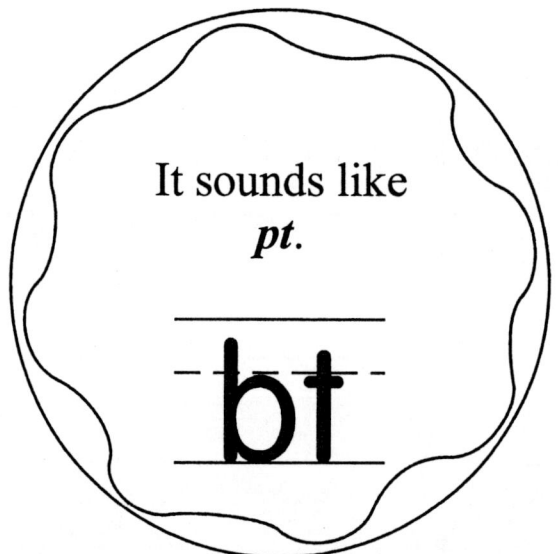

It sounds like
ps.

_____
bs

It sounds like
su.

_____
su

It sounds like
ay-oo.

_____
eu

It sounds like
pt.

_____
bt

☐ I practiced my flashcards today.

SPECIAL CONSONANTS

Draw a line from the special consonants to their sounds.

ph in *phone*   i
su in *suave*   su
y in *youth*   ph

th

sounds like
th in *thick*

Write the consonants th across each line.
As you write them, say the "**th**" sound in *thick*.

th   th   th   th

th   th   th   th

☐ I practiced my flashcards today.
(Remember to add this new card to your flashcards.)

REMEMBER!
th sounds like **th** in *thick*.

Draw a line from each kite to its roll of string.

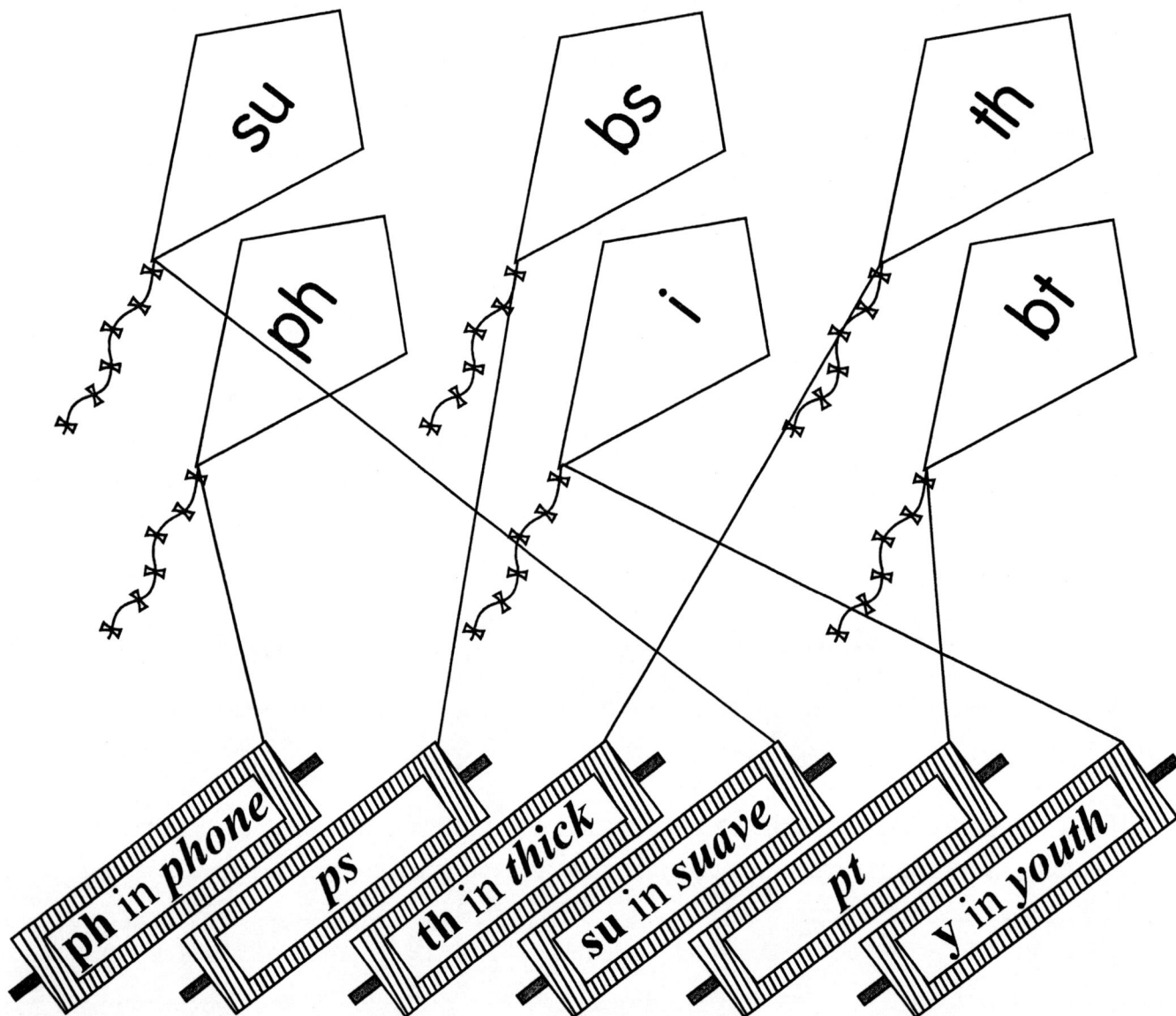

su

bs

th

ph

i

bt

ph in *phone*

ps

th in *thick*

su in *suave*

pt

y in *youth*

☐ I practiced my flashcards today.

LET'S PRACTICE

Match the Latin letters with their sounds.

gu   **th** in *thick*

ui   **gu** in *anguish*

th   **ph** in *phone*

ei   **uee** in *queen*

ph   **ei** in *neighbor*

ch   **su** in *suave*

i   **oy** in *joy*

su   **ch** in *character*

oe   **y** in *youth*

☐ I practiced my flashcards today.

LET'S PRACTICE

Color the triangle if the Latin letters match the sound.

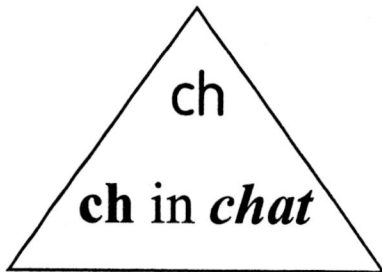

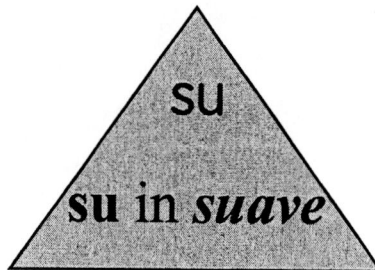

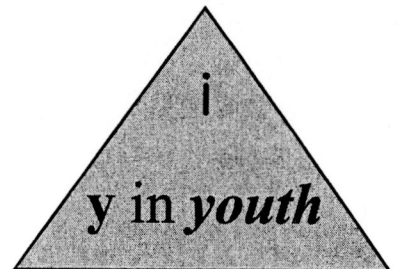

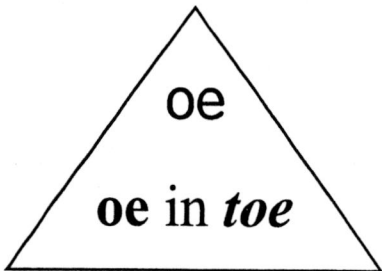

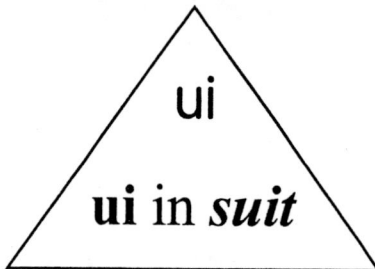

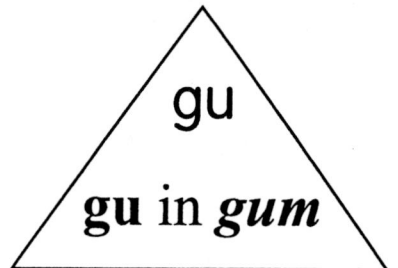

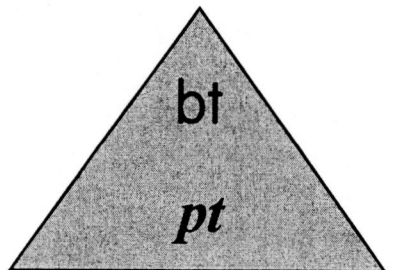

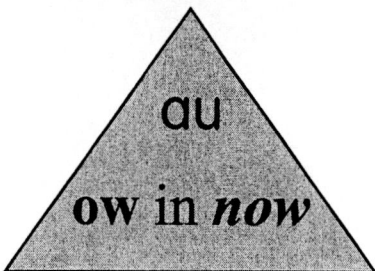

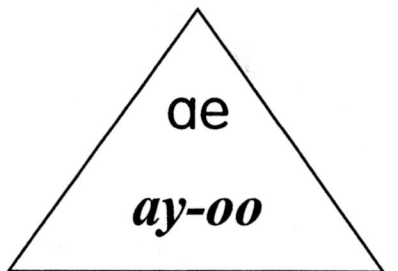

ch
ch in *chat*

su
su in *suave*

i
y in *youth*

oe
oe in *toe*

ui
ui in *suit*

gu
gu in *gum*

ei
ie in *pie*

th
th in *thick*

bt
pt

ph
ph in *phone*

au
ow in *now*

ae
ay-oo

☐ I practiced my flashcards today.

LET'S PRACTICE

Draw a line from each pickle to its jar.

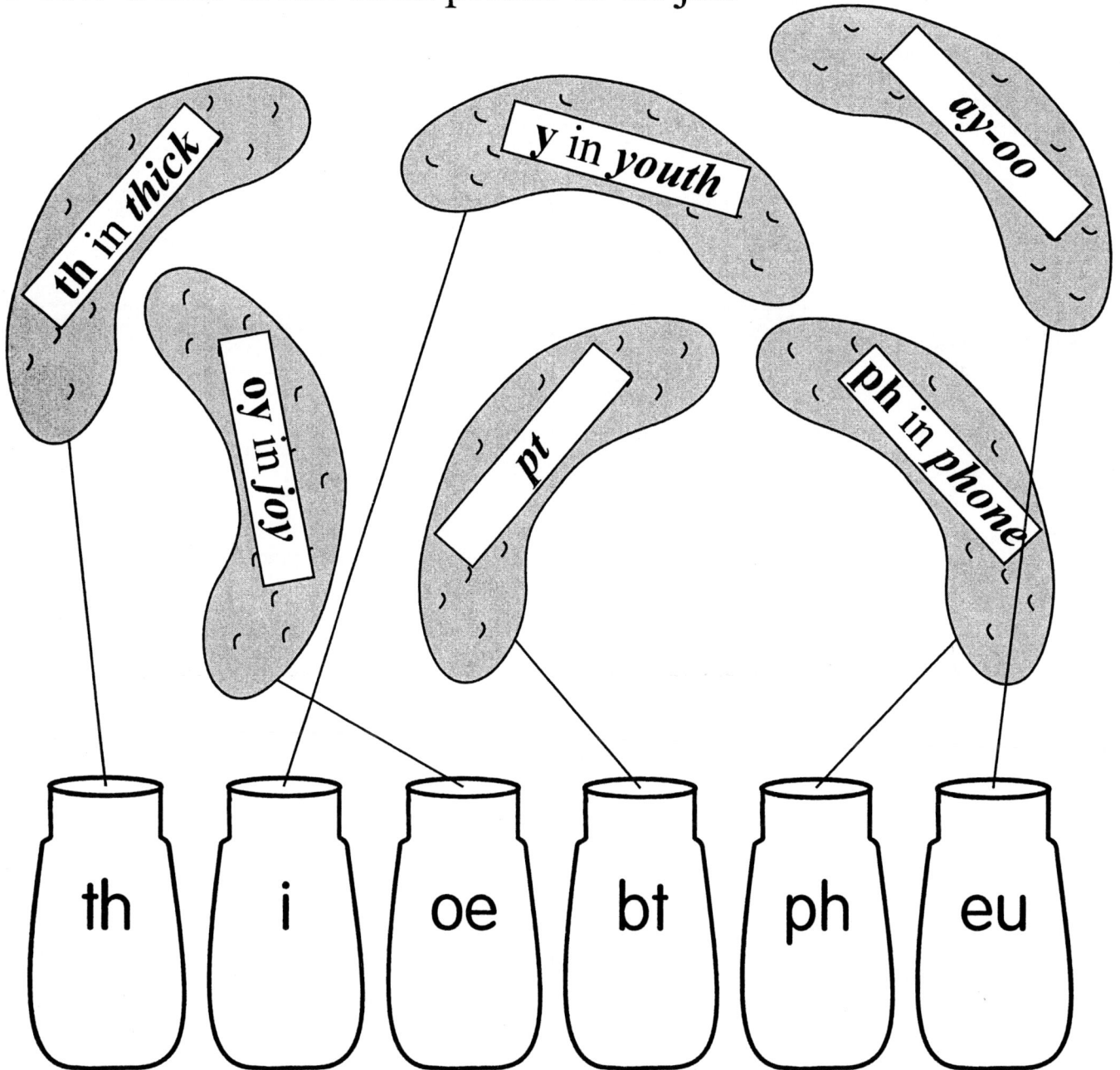

th in *thick*

y in *youth*

ay-oo

oy in *joy*

pt

ph in *phone*

th   i   oe   bt   ph   eu

☐   I practiced my flashcards today.

LET'S PRACTICE

Look at the Latin letters in the corner of the box.
Circle the words that have the sound they make.

oe
sew
toe
(boy)
(enjoy)
(coin)

su
(swim)
sun
sue
(swan)
(sweep)

ch
chess
(ache)
(chrome)
arch
(anchor)

bs
(lips)
(caps)
ribs
tubs
(tops)

th
(thimble)
(throne)
this
that
(thank)

ei
(eight)
receive
weird
(stay)
(rain)

☐ I practiced my flashcards today.

96

LET'S PRACTICE

Fill in the blanks with the missing lowercase Latin letters.

1. Latin **su** sounds like the **su** in *suave*.

2. Latin **gu** sounds like the **gu** in *anguish*.

3. Latin **ei** sounds like the **ei** in *neighbor*.

4. Latin **th** sounds like the **th** in *thick*.

5. Latin **ph** sounds like the **ph** in *phone*.

6. Latin **ch** sounds like the **ch** in *character*.

☐ I practiced my flashcards today.

LET'S PRACTICE

Circle the correct Latin letters below each sound.

ks in *socks*		w in *way*		u in *put*	
kz	(x)	(v)	u	ū	(u)
uee in *queen*		**oy in *joy***		***ps***	
(ui)	ē	oy	(oe)	ps	(bs)
pt		**y in *youth***		***ay-oo***	
pt	(bt)	y	(i)	(eu)	ao
aye		**ow in *now***		**ei in *neighbor***	
(ae)	ay	ov	(au)	ā	(ei)
c in *cat*		**i in *machine***		**o in *note***	
(c)	s	(ī)	i	(ō)	o

☐ I practiced my flashcards today.

LET'S PRACTICE

Circle the letters that match the sound in the big box.

ay-oo	(eu)	ae	ei
e in *bet*	(e)	eu	ē
o in *omit*	oe	ō	(o)
c in *cat*	k	(c)	ch
y in *youth*	y	(i)	ȳ
u in *rule*	u	(ū)	y
pt	pt	ps	(bt)
i in *machine*	i	(ī)	y
a in *father*	a	(ā)	ae
ps	(bs)	ps	sp

☐ I practiced my flashcards today.

LET'S PRACTICE

Circle *yes* if the sentence is true. Circle *no* if it is not true.

yes *no*   1. The Latin letters ᴄh sound like the **ch** in *character*.

yes *no*   2. The Latin letters ᴜi sound like the **ui** in *suit*.

yes *no*   3. The Latin letters ᵗh sound like the **th** in *them*.

yes *no*   4. The Latin letters oe sound like the **oy** in *joy*.

yes *no*   5. The Latin letters ᵍu sound like the **gu** in *anguish*.

yes *no*   6. The Latin consonant i sounds like the **y** in *youth*.

yes *no*   7. The Latin letters bs sound like *ps.*

☐ I practiced my flashcards today.

Latin Workbook - Level 1
Copyright © 1996 by Karen Mohs

LET'S PRACTICE

Write the Latin letters for the first sound you hear in the English words.

young	i	fat	f
pig	p	thick	th
oil	oe	seed	s
last	l	Christ	ch
obey	o	barn	b
garden	g	swim	su
west	v	oats	ō

☐ I practiced my flashcards today.

LET'S PRACTICE

Draw a line from each balloon to its gingerbread boy.

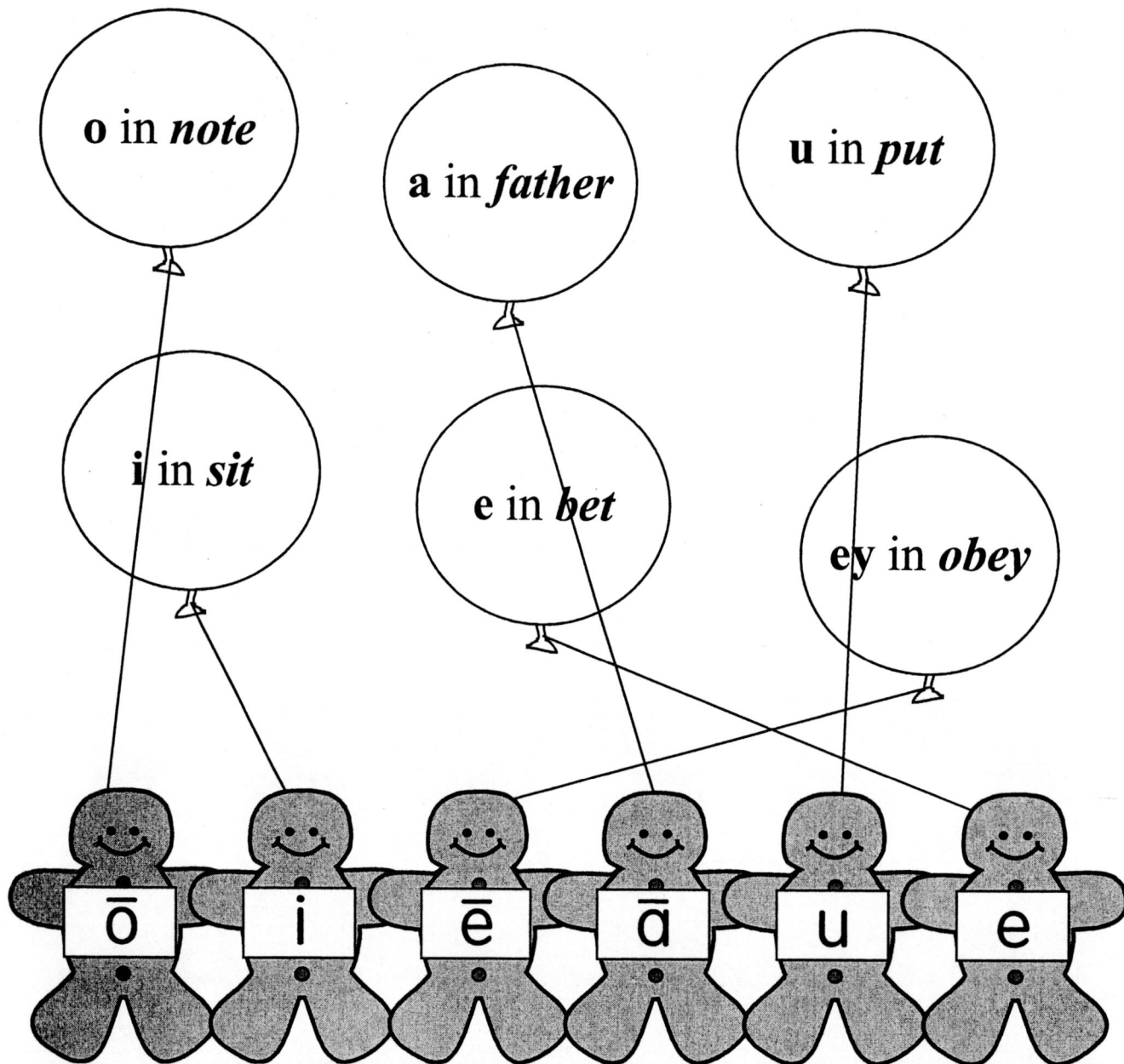

o in *note*

a in *father*

u in *put*

i in *sit*

e in *bet*

ey in *obey*

ō i ē ā u e

☐ I practiced my flashcards today.

Latin Workbook - Level 1
Copyright © 1996 by Karen Mohs

LET'S PRACTICE

Match the Latin letters with their sounds.

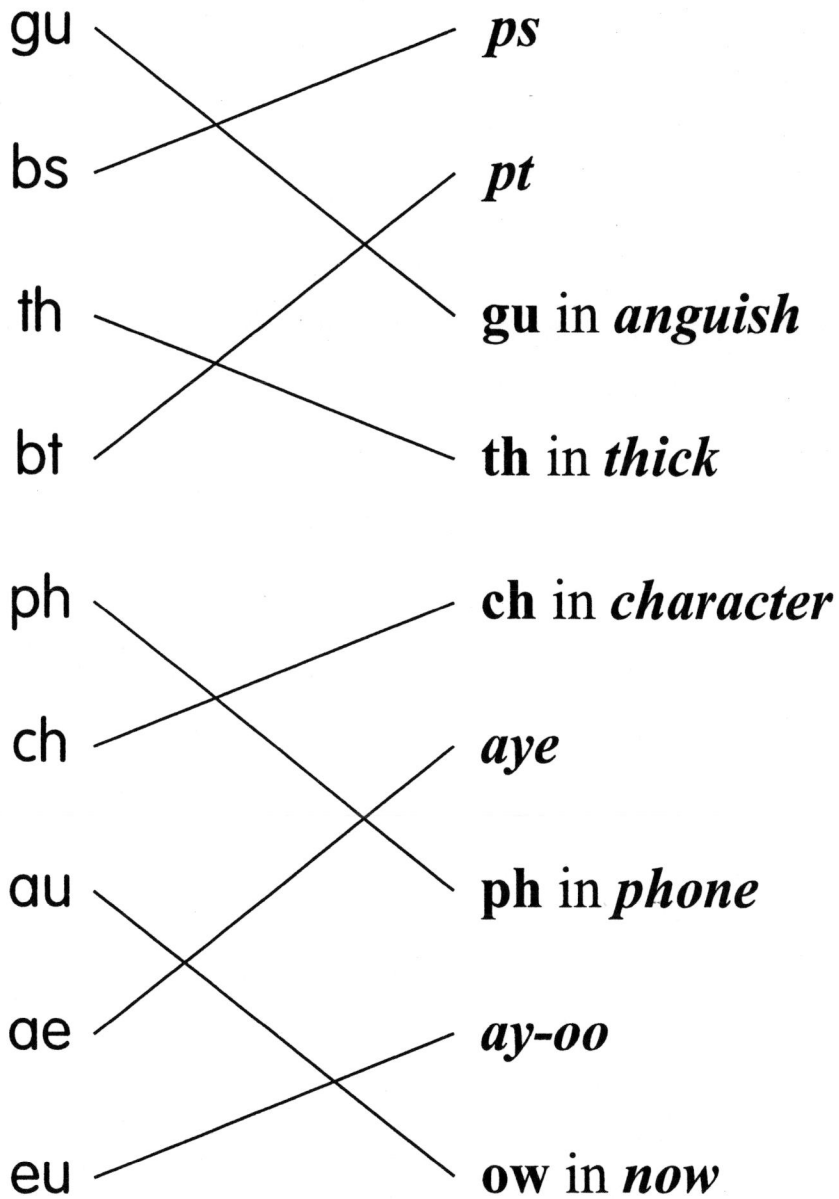

gu   *ps*

bs   *pt*

th   **gu** in *anguish*

bt   **th** in *thick*

ph   **ch** in *character*

ch   *aye*

au   **ph** in *phone*

ae   *ay-oo*

eu   **ow** in *now*

☐ I practiced my flashcards today.

LET'S PRACTICE

Fill in the blanks with the missing sounds and words.

1. Latin bt sounds like _____ pt _____ .

2. Latin gu sounds like ____ gu ____ in ____ anguish ____ .

3. Latin th sounds like ____ th ____ in ____ thick ____ .

4. Latin ph sounds like ____ ph ____ in ____ phone ____ .

5. Latin bs sounds like _____ ps _____ .

6. Latin ch sounds like ____ ch ____ in ____ character ____ .

☐ I practiced my flashcards today.

Latin Workbook - Level 1
Copyright © 1996 by Karen Mohs

APPENDIX

Latin Alphabet

Capital Letter	Small Letter	Pronunciation	Capital Letter	Small Letter	Pronunciation
Ā	ā	**a** in *father*	N	n	**n** in *nut*
A	a	**a** in *idea*	Ō**	ō**	**o** in *note*
B	b	**b** in *boy*	O**	o**	**o** in *omit*
C	c	**c** in *cat*	P	p	**p** in *pit*
D	d	**d** in *dog*	Q	q	**qu** in *quit*
Ē	ē	**ey** in *obey*	R	r	**r** in *run*
E	e	**e** in *bet*	S	s	**s** in *sit*
F	f	**f** in *fan*	T	t	**t** in *tag*
G	g	**g** in *go*	Ū	ū	**u** in *rule*
H	h	**h** in *hat*	U	u	**u** in *put*
Ī	ī	**i** in *machine*	V	v	**w** in *way*
I*	i*	**i** in *sit*	X	x	**ks** in *socks*
K	k	**k** in *king*	Ȳ	ȳ	form lips to say "oo" but say "ee" instead (held longer)
L	l	**l** in *land*	Y	y	form lips to say "oo" but say "ee" instead (held shorter)
M	m	**m** in *man*	Z	z	**dz** in *adze*

*When functioning as a consonant, i has the sound of **y** in *youth*. (See **Special Consonants** below.)

**The ō and the o both have a long o sound, but the ō is held longer.

Special Sounds

Diphthongs

Letters	Pronunciation
ae	*aye*
au	**ow** in *now*
ei	**ei** in *neighbor*
eu	*ay-oo*
oe	**oy** in *joy*
ui	**uee** in *queen*

Special Consonants

Letters	Pronunciation
bs	*ps*
bt	*pt*
ch	**ch** in *character*
gu	**gu** in *anguish*
i	**y** in *youth*
ph	**ph** in *phone*
su	**su** in *suave*
th	**th** in *thick*

APPENDIX

Flashcard Tips

1. Remember to practice flashcards daily.

2. Do not move ahead in the workbook if your student is struggling for mastery. Review the flashcards every day until your student is confident and ready to learn more.

106

All "Full" Workbook Sets include:	Latin's Not So Tough! Order Form	All "Short" Workbook Sets include:
1 Student Workbook 1 "Full Text" Answer Key 1 Quizzes/Exams 1 "Flashcards on a Ring"		1 Student Workbook 1 "Answers Only" Answer Key 1 Quizzes/Exams 1 "Flashcards on a Ring"

Name _____

Street Address _____

City _____ State _____ Zip _____

Phone _____ E-mail Address _____

QTY	ITEM#	TITLE	PRICE EACH	TOTAL
	LA-01-SS	LNST! - Level One "Short" Workbook Set	$ 24.45	$
	LA-01-FS	LNST! - Level One "Full" Workbook Set	34.40	
	LA-01-WB	Additional Level One student workbook	12.95	
	LA-02-SS	LNST! - Level Two "Short" Workbook Set	29.45	
	LA-02-FS	LNST! - Level Two "Full" Workbook Set	42.40	
	LA-02-WB	Additional Level Two student workbook	15.95	
	LA-03-SS	LNST! - Level Three "Short" Workbook Set	33.45	
	LA-03-FS	LNST! - Level Three "Full" Workbook Set	49.40	
	LA-03-WB	Additional Level Three student workbook	18.95	
	LA-04-SS	LNST! - Level Four "Short" Workbook Set	37.45	
	LA-04-FS	LNST! - Level Four "Full" Workbook Set	55.40	
	LA-04-WB	Additional Level Four student workbook	20.95	
	LA-05-SS	LNST! - Level Five "Short" Workbook Set	37.45	
	LA-05-FS	LNST! - Level Five "Full" Workbook Set	55.40	
	LA-05-WB	Additional Level Five student workbook	20.95	
	LA-CD-123	Pronunciation CD for Levels One, Two, and Three	8.00	
	LA-TP-123	Pronunciation Tape for Levels One, Two, and Three	6.00	
	LA-CD-45	Pronunciation CD for Levels Four and Five	8.00	
	LA-TP-45	Pronunciation Tape for Levels Four and Five	6.00	

Allow 4-6 weeks for delivery. Prices are subject to change without notice. International Orders: Write or e-mail for shipping costs.

Send with payment to:
Greek 'n' Stuff
P.O. Box 882
Moline, IL 61266-0882

Subtotal	
Sales tax (IL residents)	
10% Postage/handling ($3.50 minimum)	
Total enclosed